NEXT STATION 3

STUDENT'S BOOK

Amanda Cant / Mary Charrington
Sarah Elizabeth Sprague

macmillan education

PAGES 4-5 Characters and Icons   **PAGES 6-7** World Map

Unit 1 — PAGES 8-17

VOCABULARY
exploring, climbing, dancing, watching TV, swimming, singing, playing soccer

cute, athletic, friendly, strong, funny, smart

GRAMMAR
Let's go to the …
Let's go by …

(I sit) in front of / next to / behind (Ben.)

FEATURES
Country: Mexico
World Music Song: The High Five Song
Phonics: ar, all, or

Unit 2 — PAGES 18-27

VOCABULARY
eggs, cupcakes, sausages, potato chips, cherries, strawberries, avocados, grapes

soup, rice, bread, cereal, milk, soda, chocolate, pasta

GRAMMAR
There are some … -s.
There aren't any … -s.

There's some …
There isn't any …
Is there any … ?
Yes, there is. / No, there isn't.

FEATURES
Country: South Africa
World Music Song: No Sausages!
Phonics: br, sn, cl

PAGES 28-29 Progress Check Units 1 & 2   **PAGES 30-31** Steam Challenge 1

Unit 3 — PAGES 32-41

VOCABULARY
Turkey, Turkish, South Korea, South Korean, Malaysia, Malaysian, the USA, American, Spain, Spanish, Japan, Japanese, the UK, British, India, Indian

eat, drink, cook, sleep, wash, write

GRAMMAR
Where are you from?
I'm / We're from …
He's / She's / It's from …
He's / She's / It's (nationality).

Play with me / us.
Can I dance with you?
Let's dance with him / her / them.
Climb it.

FEATURES
Country: Malaysia
World Music Song: Travel Song
Phonics: fr, bl, lk

Unit 4 — PAGES 42-51

VOCABULARY
ride, dive, climb, surf, fish, skate, ski, skateboard

ping pong, tennis, baseball, soccer, ice hockey, basketball

GRAMMAR
I'm / We're … -ing.
I'm not … -ing.
We aren't … -ing.

Are you / they … -ing?
Yes, I am. / No, I'm not.
Yes, they are. / No, they aren't.

FEATURES
Country: Italy
World Music Song: Cool Sports
Phonics: sk, sw, str

PAGES 52-53 Progress Check Units 3 & 4   **PAGES 54-55** Steam Challenge 2

Unit 5 — PAGES 56-65

VOCABULARY
hot, rainy, sunny, cold, foggy, cloudy, windy, snowy

dress, shorts, T-shirt, jeans, socks, boots

GRAMMAR
What's he / she / it doing?
He's / She's / It's … -ing.
He / She / It isn't … -ing.

Is he / she … -ing?
Yes, he / she is. / No, he / she isn't.

FEATURES
Country: Jamaica
World Music Song: The Island Song
Phonics: oo, ir, ow

UNIT 6 — PAGES 66-75

VOCABULARY
hospital, museum, café, movie theater, airport, supermarket, library, farm

cousin, baby brother, baby sister, uncle, aunt, grandparents

GRAMMAR
Are you / they going to the … ?
Yes, I am / we are.
No, I'm not / we aren't.

Where is he / she going?
He's / She's going to …
Is he / she / it going to … ?
Yes, he / she is. / No, he / she isn't.

FEATURES
Country: Chile
World Music Song: The Busy, Busy Song
Phonics: er, ear, ore

PAGES 76-77 **Progress Check Units 5 & 6**   PAGES 78-79 **Steam Challenge 3**

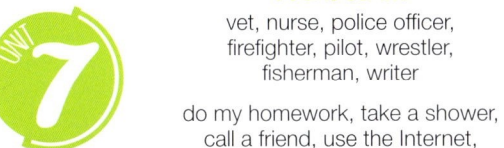

UNIT 7 — PAGES 80-89

VOCABULARY
vet, nurse, police officer, firefighter, pilot, wrestler, fisherman, writer

do my homework, take a shower, call a friend, use the Internet, brush my teeth, buy candy

GRAMMAR
I'm (not) going to be a …
Are you going to be a … ?
Yes, I am. / No, I'm not.

He / She's going to …
He / She isn't going to …
Is he / she going to … ?
Yes, he / she is. / No, he / she isn't.

FEATURES
Country: France
World Music Song: School Days
Phonics: ur, or, a

UNIT 8 — PAGES 90-99

VOCABULARY
January, February, March, April, May, June, July, August, September, October, November, December

happy, sad, tired, bored, excited, scared, mad

GRAMMAR
I was / They were born in (month).
I was / They were born in a hospital / at home.
Were you / they born … ?
Yes, I was / they were. / No, I wasn't / they weren't.

You / They were … / weren't …

FEATURES
Country: USA
World Music Song: In Your Dreams
Phonics: dr, ld, gr

PAGES 100-101 **Progress Check Units 7 & 8**   PAGES 102-103 **Steam Challenge 4**

UNIT 9 — PAGES 104-113

VOCABULARY
thirty, a quarter after, a quarter to, midnight, noon

picnic, birthday party, wedding, barbecue, parade

GRAMMAR
I / He / She / It was …
I / He / She / It wasn't …

Was he / she / it … ?
Yes, he / she / it was.
No, he / she / it wasn't.

FEATURES
Country: Morocco
World Music Song: The Mystery Song
Phonics: air, ou, oy

UNIT 10 — PAGES 114-123

VOCABULARY
furniture, toys, animals, food, money, clothes

spring, summer, fall, winter, snow, ice, water

GRAMMAR
There was some furniture.
There was a horse.
There were some flowers.

How much … was there?
How many … were there?

FEATURES
Country: Vietnam
World Music Song: Last Summer
Phonics: sm, sc, tr

PAGES 124-125 **Progress Check Units 9 & 10**   PAGES 126-127 **Steam Challenge 5**

PAGE 128 **GRAMMAR GUIDE**

Hi! My name's Zac. Do you like exploring? I do! Are you ready to go places? Are you ready to learn English?

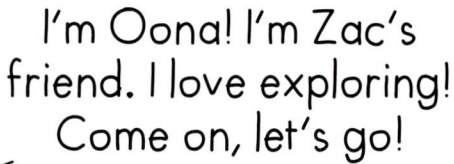

I'm Oona! I'm Zac's friend. I love exploring! Come on, let's go!

Activities to interpret the picture of the unit opener pages

LISTEN
Audio tracks to practice listening skills

WORLD MUSIC
Songs with a World Music flavor

TEMPLATE
Photocopiable Language File activities to use in class

BE sociable and creative. Know yourself!

THINK critically when you use information!

LEARN to do things by yourself. Learn how to learn!

COLLABORATE / COMMUNICATE with others. Teamwork is cool!

ACT respectfully, be tolerant and friendly!

WELCOME TO NEXT STATION!

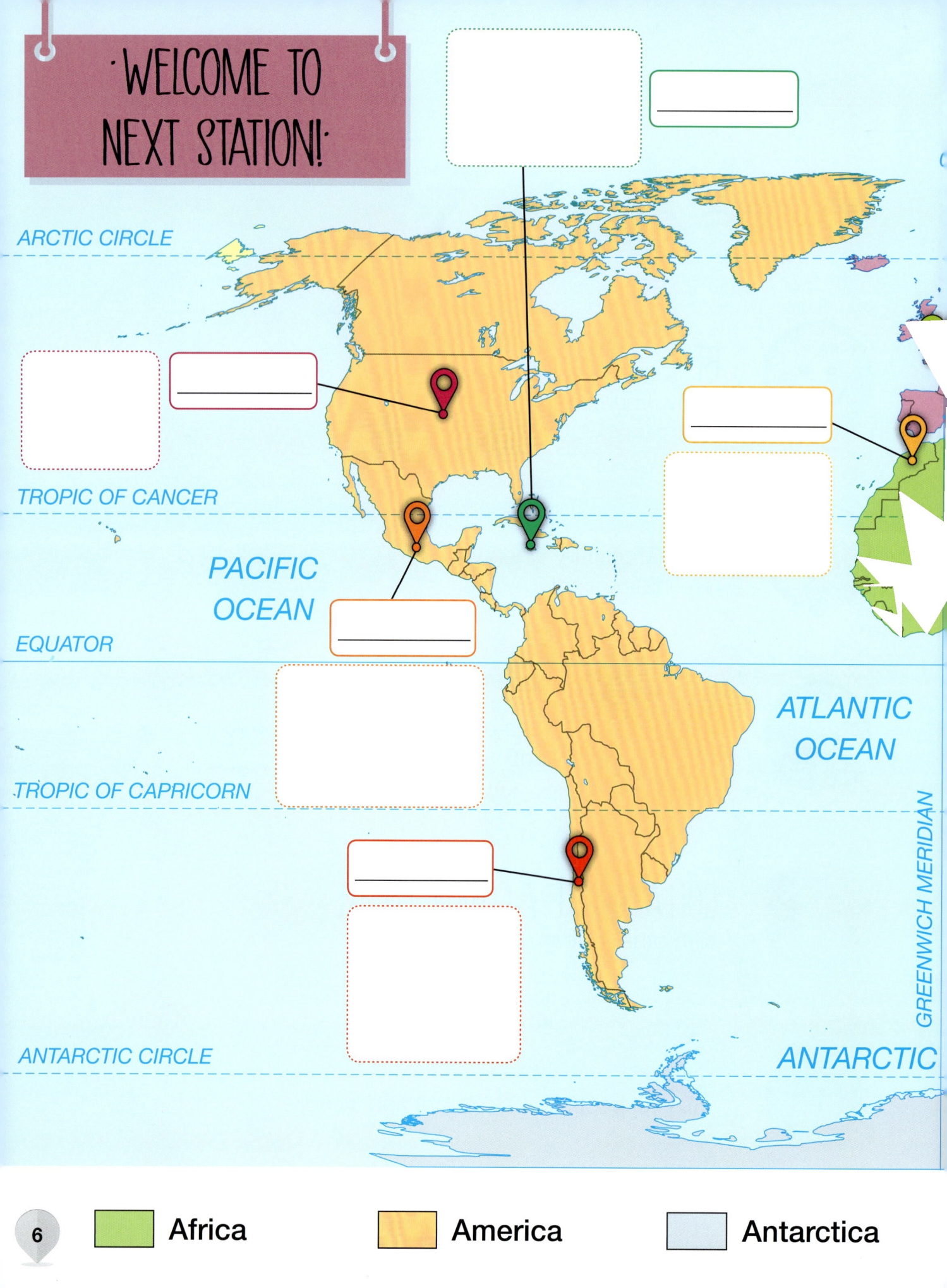

ARCTIC CIRCLE

TROPIC OF CANCER

PACIFIC OCEAN

EQUATOR

ATLANTIC OCEAN

TROPIC OF CAPRICORN

GREENWICH MERIDIAN

ANTARCTIC CIRCLE

ANTARCTIC

Africa America Antarctica

ARCTIC OCEAN

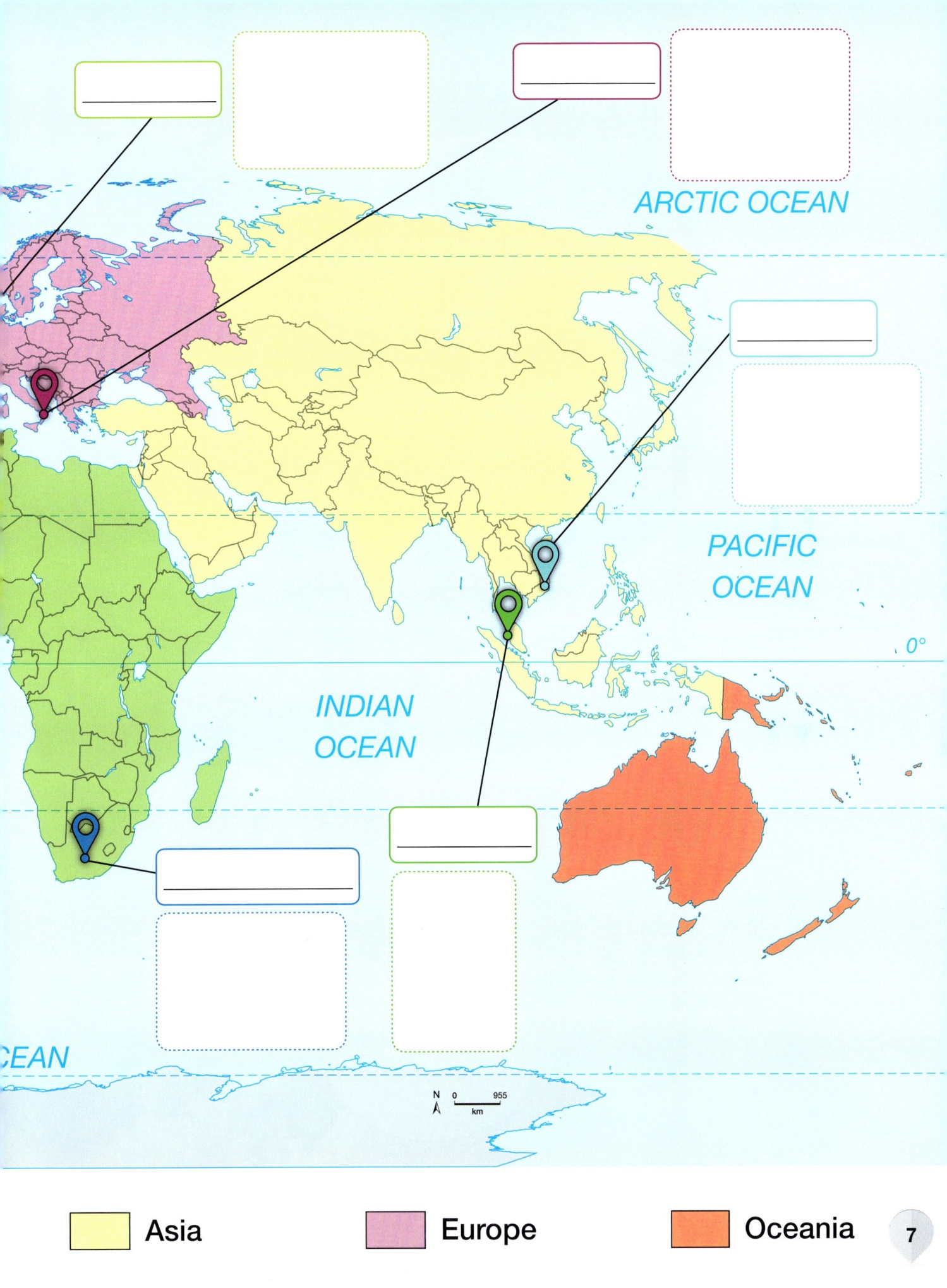

PACIFIC OCEAN

INDIAN OCEAN

0°

Asia   Europe   Oceania

7

MEXICO

UNIT 1

Welcome to Mexico!

We like exploring. Let's explore the ocean.

The *diver is* in the Pacific Ocean in Mexico!

What are the five oceans in the world?
Which ocean creatures do you know?
Do you live near the ocean?

ZOOM IN

Look at the picture.
Can you think of three things the diver can see?

UNIT 1

Lesson 1

VOCABULARY

TRACK 2

1 Listen and read.

1
Hi, Oona. How are you?
I'm fine, thanks.

2
I like exploring.
Me too!

2 Check (✓) the activities you like. Then say.

○ exploring
○ swimming
○ climbing
○ singing

○ dancing
○ playing soccer
○ watching TV

WORKBOOK page 4

Lesson 2

GRAMMAR

Let's go to the desert.
Let's go by bus.

TRACK 3

1 Listen, read, and say.

1. Let's go to the desert and ride a donkey.
2. OK. Let's go by train. / Let's go by bus. / Let's go by plane!
3. Good idea!

DISCOVER GRAMMAR

Circle.
Let's go **by** + **place / transportation**.
Let's go **to** + **place / transportation**.

TRACK 4

2 Listen and say *Let's go by …* or *Let's go to …*

3 Complete and say.

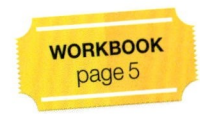

1. Let's go _____.
2. Let's go _____.
3. Let's go _____.
4. Let's go _____.

WORKBOOK page 5 · GRAMMAR GUIDE page 129

UNIT 1

Lesson 3 — SOUNDS AND SPELLING

ar all or

TRACK 5

1 Listen and chant.

I'm in the park.
I have a guitar!

I'm in the mall.
I have a new ball.

Where am I this morning?
I'm exploring!

TRACK 6

2 Listen and complete. Then cross (✗) out the word with a different sound.

1. guit _a_ _r_
   m __ __ __
   b __ __ __
   _____

2. m __ __ ning
   expl __ __ ing
   p __ __ k
   _____

3. m __ __ __
   p __ __ k
   guit __ __
   _____

3 Add one more word to each column.

WORKBOOK page 6

Lesson 4 ·READING TIME·

TRACK 7

1 Listen and read.

1. Please don't run in the mall.
2. Hey! Don't drop litter in the park!
3. Sit down, Marty.
4. Ouch!

2 Read the story again. Check (✓) the **value**.

Respect: Listen to others. ○   Listen to yourself. ○

3 Think and answer.

Are you good at listening to others? Circle.   Yes / No

Who do you listen to? _____ _____ _____

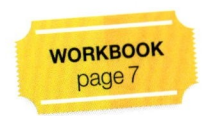

WORKBOOK page 7

UNIT 1

Lesson 5

VOCABULARY

TRACK 8

1 Listen, point, and say.

1. cute
2. athletic  
3. friendly 
4. smart 
5. funny 
6. strong 

2 Put the words into the correct column.

physical appearance	characteristics

TRACK 9

3 Listen and sing. Then make a new verse. **The High Five Song**

Let's High Five!
I'm smart,
You're smart,
We're all smart today.

Friends are smart!
Friends are cool,
Let's be friends,
At our school.

Let's High Five!
I'm strong,
You're strong,
We're all strong today.

_____
_____
_____
_____

WORKBOOK page 8

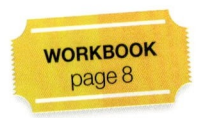

14

Lesson 6

TRACK 10

1. Listen, read, and say.

Zac is on a plane, and he can see lots of things. There's a city next to the ocean. There's a jungle behind the city, and there's a pyramid in front of a mountain.

GRAMMAR

The city is **next to** the ocean.
The jungle is **behind** the city.
The pyramid is **in front of** the mountain.

But he can't see Oona under the plane.

DISCOVER GRAMMAR

Read. Then circle.
Alan sits **behind** me and **next to** Ben.
The sentence is talking about **time / place**.

2. Look and write.

1 Where is the city? _____.

2 Where is the jungle? _____.

3 Where is the pyramid? _____.

3. Play the Guessing Game.

This person is friendly. She sits behind Al.

It's Sofia.

WORKBOOK page 9

GRAMMAR GUIDE page 129

Lesson 7

FACTUAL READER

LET'S VISIT MEXICO

1 Read about green iguanas from Mexico.

Green iguanas are lizards, and they live in Mexico. They aren't very friendly, but they're smart, and they're strong, too. They can climb trees and they can swim. They have short legs, a big head, and a very long tongue. They like eating leaves, flowers, and fruit for breakfast, lunch, and dinner!

It's a fact!
Green iguanas can be two meters long! How tall are you?

2 Find out and write about green iguanas.

- characteristics
- abilities
- habits
- physical appearance

Think Twice

1. Do you like iguanas? Do you think they're interesting?
2. Why do you think these iguanas are green and brown?

Lesson 8

SPEAKING TIME

PRESENTATION: AN ANIMAL FROM YOUR COUNTRY

1. Prepare.

Find information about your animal.

- Choose an animal from your country.
- Draw a picture and label it.
- Find information about it.

characteristics	
abilities	
habits	
physical appearance	

2. Practice.

Describe your animal.

- Let me tell you about …
- They live in …
- They have …
- They like eating …
- They can …
- They can't …

TRACK 11

3. Present.

Let me tell you about brown bears. They live in the mountains. They have big bodies and strong legs. They like eating fish and small mammals. They can swim, but they can't climb trees.

Brown Bears

WORKBOOK page 10

SOUTH AFRICA

SOUTH AFRICA

UNIT 2

We're in South Africa. Look at the beautiful giraffe.

This giraffe lives in South Africa.

What other countries do giraffes live in?
What is the giraffe eating?
What else does it eat?
Do you have giraffes in your country?

ZOOM IN

Look at the picture.
Why do you think giraffes have long necks?

Lesson 1

· VOCABULARY ·

TRACK 12

1 Listen, point, and say.

1 strawberries
2 cherries
3 avocados
4 grapes
5 potato chips
6 eggs
7 sausages
8 cupcakes

2 Write sentences using *I like* and *I don't like*.

☺
1 I like . . .
2 _____
3 _____
4 _____

☹
5 I don't like . . .
6 _____
7 _____
8 _____

3 Talk to a friend.

Cupcakes!

Do you like cupcakes?

C-u-p-c-a-k-e-s.

Yes, I do.

20

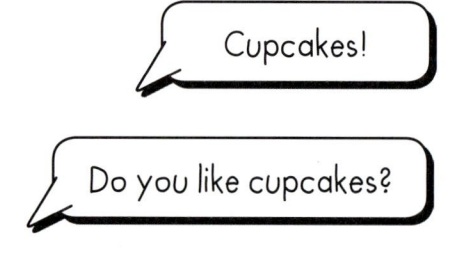

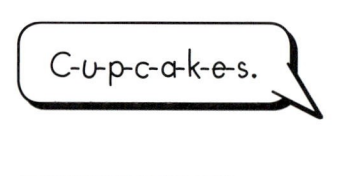

WORKBOOK page 11

Lesson 2

GRAMMAR

There are some sausages.
There aren't any cherries.

TRACK 13

1 Listen, read, and say.

Zac and Oona are on safari and it's time for lunch.

Look at this picnic! There are some sausages and some sandwiches.

There aren't any strawberries, and there aren't any cherries.

But there are some lions!

DISCOVER GRAMMAR

Circle.

There's + **some** / **any** …

There isn't + **some** / **any** …

2 Look at Activity 1. Then complete the sentences with *are some* or *aren't any*.

1 There _____ apples.

2 There _____ cupcakes.

3 There _____ eggs.

4 There _____ pears.

3 Play the Memory Game.

There are some sausages.

Yes!

WORKBOOK page 12

GRAMMAR GUIDE page 129

21

Lesson 3 — SOUNDS AND SPELLING

TRACK 14

1 Listen and chant.

br sn cl

Sara gets up at seven o'clock.
It's a very cloudy day.
For breakfast she has bread.
She's hungry today!

Sara's at the library.
Brian the snake is there.
They read a book and have a snack,
Some cupcakes and a pear.

2 Circle, sort, and write.

breakfastsnacksnakeclockcloudylibrary

br	sn	cl
_____	_____	_____
_____	_____	_____

3 Write a word with *br*, *sn*, or *cl*.

❶ brown

❷ _____

❸ _____

WORKBOOK page 13

Lesson 4 ·READING TIME·

TRACK 15

1 Listen and read.

1 Clara gets up at 7 o'clock and has breakfast.
There are strawberries and cherries for breakfast.

2 In the morning, she has a snack.

3 Clara has lunch at 1 o'clock.
There's some soup and bread for lunch.

4 Then, she has *another* snack.
Yummy! Cupcakes!

5 She has dinner at 6 o'clock.
Mmm. Sausages, potatoes, and beans.

6 Later, Clara is in bed.
One snack a day, OK?

2 Read the story again. Check (✓) the **value**.

Responsibility: Don't be greedy. ◯   Don't be lazy. ◯

3 How many snacks do you eat in a day? What are they?

Write a list of your snacks for one day and decide if you are greedy.

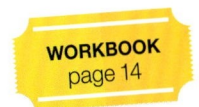

WORKBOOK page 14

Lesson 5

·VOCABULARY·

TRACK 16

1 Listen, point, and say.

1 chocolate
2 soup
3 bread
4 rice
5 cereal
6 pasta
7 milk
8 soda

2 Complete the sentences.

1 The _____ is next to the soda.
2 The _____ and the _____ are on the table.
3 The _____ is under the rice.
4 The _____ is next to the pasta.

3 Write the foods and say.

| soup   pancakes   rice   apples   bread   cereal   sandwiches |
| potatoes   milk   fish   eggs   pasta   juice   tomatoes   soda |

In my house, we have _____ for breakfast.

In my house, we have _____ for lunch.

In my house, we have _____ for dinner.

In my house, we have cereal for breakfast.

WORKBOOK page 15

24

Lesson 6

GRAMMAR

There's some / There isn't any …
Is there any rice?
Yes, there is. / No, there isn't.

TRACK 17

1 Listen, read, and say.

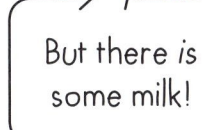

It's 8 o'clock and it's dinner time.

Mmm, there's pasta and there's fruit.

There isn't any soda.

But there *is* some milk!

DISCOVER GRAMMAR

Circle.

There's + **some** / **any** …
There isn't + **some** / **any** …
Is there + **some** / **any** … ?

2 Ask and answer.

Is there any …?   Yes, there is. / No, there isn't.

1 chocolate   2 milk   3 cereal   4 bread   5 soup   6 rice

TRACK 18

3 Listen and sing. **No Sausages!**

There aren't any sausages,
There isn't any rice,
There aren't any potato chips,
And I think they're nice!
But …

Chorus
There are some eggs, 1, 2, 3,
And there is some bread,
Just for me!

Lesson 7

FACTUAL READER

LET'S VISIT SOUTH AFRICA

1 Read about food in South Africa.

It's a fact!
One ostrich egg weighs the same as about 24 chicken eggs!

Big breakfast

Many children all over the world have cereal, toast, and eggs for breakfast. But in South Africa, if you go to an ostrich farm, there are omelets on the breakfast menu – very big omelets made from ostrich eggs! Ostrich eggs taste the same as chicken eggs, but they have very hard shells. You can jump on an ostrich egg, and it won't break! Children in South Africa eat really delicious and healthy food for lunch and dinner. There are traditional meat, chicken, and fish dishes and lots of healthy snacks like cherries, strawberries, and grapes.

2 Find and write.

1. What three things do many children have for breakfast?
2. Why are some omelets special in South Africa?
3. What snacks do South African children eat?

Think Twice

1. Compare your breakfast with a South African breakfast. Are they similar? What's different?
2. Why do you think it is important for ostrich eggs to have such hard shells?

Lesson 8

·SPEAKING TIME·

PRESENTATION: A MEAL IN YOUR COUNTRY.

1 Prepare.

Find information about the meal.

- Choose a typical meal from your country.
- Draw a picture and label it.
- Find information about it.

ingredients	taste	special characteristics

2 Practice.

Describe your typical meal.

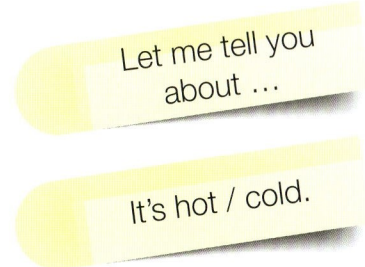

- Let me tell you about …
- It has … in it.
- It's hot / cold.
- It's salty / sweet.

TRACK 19

3 Present.

Let me tell you about my favorite breakfast – it's delicious. It's cereal, and there's some fruit in it – like strawberries or maybe some cherries. It has some bread with butter. To drink, I have some apple juice – it's nice and sweet. My breakfast is yummy!

Breakfast

WORKBOOK page 17

PROGRESS CHECK

1 Unscramble and write. /4

1 go by Let's boat. _____
2 by go car Let's. _____
3 train Let's go by. _____
4 go the to jungle Let's. _____

2 Read and write *Yes* or *No*. /6

1 There's a closet in front of the board. _____
2 There's a clock next to the window. _____
3 There's a board behind the desks. _____
4 There are two books next to the pencil case. _____
5 There's a school bag in front of a chair. _____
6 There's a trash can behind the door. _____

TOTAL /10

WORKBOOK page 18   STICKERS   PASSPORT page 2

· PROGRESS CHECK ·

1 Read the story and write the words.   /5

Billy is a very greedy boy. Today he has a big breakfast. He has some

1 _____cereal_____ with milk, then some fruit – some

2 _____. At school, he has a snack. He has

some 3 _____ and some orange juice. For lunch,

he has potatoes, beans, and some 4 _____.

After school, he has four 5 _____ and a

6 _____. Then Billy feels sick!

2 Look at the picture and write sentences.   /5

There's some …   There isn't any …   There are some …   There aren't any …

1 _____There's some_____ bread.
2 _____ milk.
3 _____ ice cream.
4 _____ sandwiches.
5 _____ potato chips.
6 _____ soup.

TOTAL   /10

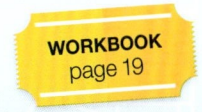

WORKBOOK page 19   **STICKERS**   **PASSPORT** page 4

MEXICO

Mexican kids playing soccer in Guanajuato.

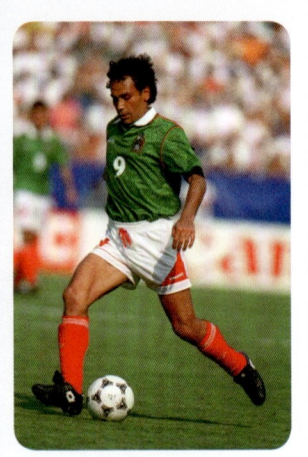

Hugo Sanchez, a famous Mexican soccer player, at the 1994 World Cup.

Mexican fan at a 2010 World Cup match.

STEAM

TEAM NAME

Can you name some different kinds of balls?

1 Get materials.

- paper
- 25-30 plastic bags
- string
- rubber bands

Super Star Challenge

2 Make a small paper ball and put it in a plastic bag.

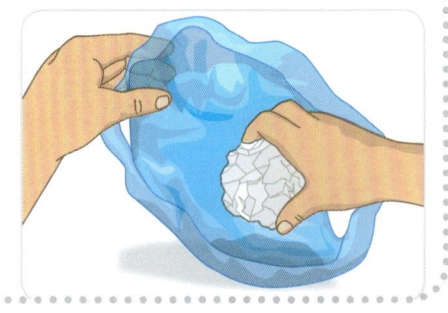

The ancient Mayan civilization used a heavy ball to play a game called *pok-ta-pok*.

In South Africa, there is a century old sport played with a ball. It's called ringball.

CHALLENGE 1

MAKE A BALL

SOUTH AFRICA

3 Twist the end of the bag and cover the ball again.

4 Tie the handles of the bag together and repeat the process with all the plastic bags.

5 Tie some strings around the ball and play.

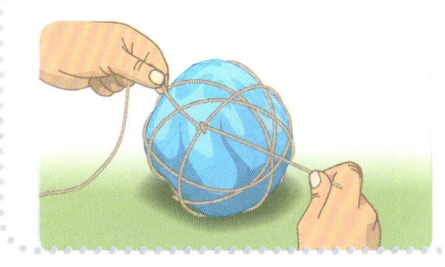

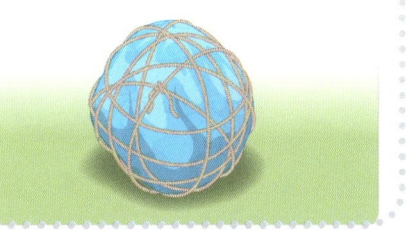

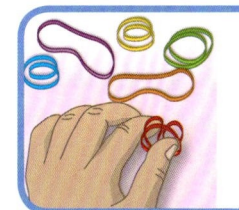

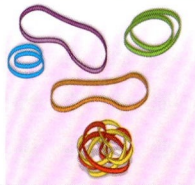

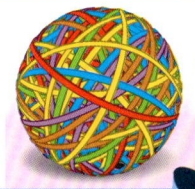

A plastic bag takes 450 years to decompose. How can you reuse it?

Super Star Challenge
Make a rubber band ball.

Soccer is one of the most popular sports in South Africa.

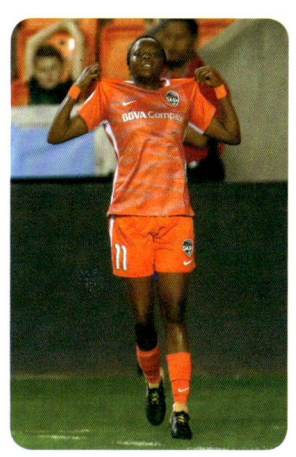

Thembi Kgatlana, named the best women's soccer player in Africa.

Plastic horns are very popular at the games.

TEAMWORK ★★★★☆

31

MALAYSIA

ARRIVAL
MALAYSIA
06 OCT

Look! It's the Festival of Colors. Wow!

Unit 3

I'm from Malaysia.

This is a traditional Malaysian festival.

What countries are next to Malaysia on a map? Find a map and look.
Do you know about any traditional festivals in your country?
Do you ever wear traditional costumes? When?

ZOOM IN
Look at the picture.
What colors do you see?

Lesson 1

·VOCABULARY·

TRACK 20

1 Listen, point, and say.

1	Turkey	Turkish
2	South Korea	South Korean
3	Malaysia	Malaysian
4	the USA	American
5	Spain	Spanish
6	Japan	Japanese
7	the UK	British
8	India	Indian

2 Complete the sentences.

1 The _____ and the _____ flags are red and white.

2 The _____ and the _____ flags are red, blue, and white.

3 The _____ flag is red, blue, white, and yellow.

4 The _____ flag is orange, green, white, and blue.

3 Talk about a flag with your friend.

This flag is from Malaysia.

It's red, blue, white, and yellow.

WORKBOOK page 20

Lesson 2

GRAMMAR
Where are you from?
I'm from Mexico. **I'm** Mexican.
Where's he / she from?
He's / She's from Spain.
He's / She's Spanish.

TRACK 21

1 Listen, read, and say.

Hi. I'm from Malaysia. Where are you from?

I'm from the USA. This is Oona. She's Malaysian, too.

We're from Malaysia!

DISCOVER GRAMMAR

Circle.
We're from + **Turkey** / **Turkish**.
We're + **Turkey** / **Turkish**.

2 Circle. Then ask and answer.

1 Where are pandas from?   They're from   India. / China.
2 Where are hamburgers from?   They're from   the USA. / Turkey.
3 Where's origami from?   It's from   Japan. / Russia.

3 Complete.

❶ _____Where is_____ he _____from_____?
He's from _____. He's _____.

❷ _____ they _____?
They're from _____. They're _____.

WORKBOOK page 21   GRAMMAR GUIDE page 130   35

Lesson 3 — SOUNDS AND SPELLING

TRACK 22

1 Listen and chant.

`fr` `bl` `lk`

Freddie the frog is a friendly frog from France.

Blackie is a black and blue bird.

Wilkie makes milkshakes like silk! Mmm!

TRACK 23

2 Listen and complete. Then cross (X) out the word with a different sound.

1 mi _l_ _k_ shake
   ___ ___ og
   ___ ___ iendly
   _____

2 ___ ___ ack
   ___ ___ iendly
   ___ ___ ue
   _____

3 mi ___ ___ shake
   si ___ ___
   ___ ___ ack
   _____

3 Look at the chant. Find one more word for each column.

WORKBOOK page 22

Lesson 4 ·READING TIME·

TRACK 24

1 Listen and read.

1
INTERNATIONAL STUDENTS WELCOME

Welcome to the party. Where are you from?

We're from China.

We're from Russia.

We're from Kenya.

2
I like your blue silk dress.

Thank you. I like your black bag.

Thanks! Where are you from?

I'm from India.

3
Oh ... Where are you from?

We're from Mars.

Well, you're welcome, too. We're all friends here!

2 Read again. Check (✓) the **value**.

Diversity: Talk to friendly people. ◯   Welcome different people. ◯

3 How do you welcome new people? Read and check (✓).

Say *hello* and your name. ◯   Help them with new things. ◯

Look at them. ◯   Invite them to a party. ◯

WORKBOOK page 23

Lesson 5 · VOCABULARY ·

TRACK 25

1 Listen, point, and say.

1. eat
2. cook 
3. wash 
4. drink 
5. sleep 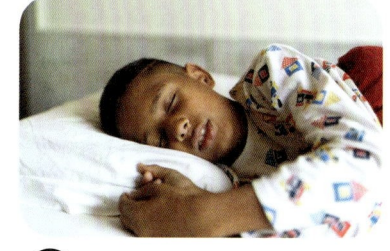
6. write 

TRACK 26

2 Listen and answer *Yes, I do* or *No, I don't*.

3 Complete the survey. Then talk to the class.

	me	friend 1	friend 2
Do you eat lunch at school?			
Do you drink milk for breakfast?			
Do you cook your dinner every day?			
Do you sleep with the door open?			
Do you wash your hair every day?			
Do you write in English every day?			

We eat our lunch at school. I drink milk for breakfast. Maria doesn't drink milk for breakfast.

WORKBOOK page 24

Lesson 6

GRAMMAR

Play with **me** / **us**.
Let's dance with **him** / **her** / **them**.
Climb **it**.

TRACK 27

1 Listen, read, and say.

1. Look at that mountain! Let's climb it.

2. Look at those girls. Let's dance with them.
   - Can we dance with you?
   - Yes. Dance with us!

3. Look at that boy. Let's play soccer with him.
   - Come on! Play soccer with me!

4. Look at that girl. Let's help her.

5. What a busy day!

DISCOVER GRAMMAR

Check (✓).

○ They like
I / you / he / she / it / we / they.

○ They like
me / you / him / her / it / us / them.

TRACK 28

2 Listen and complete. Then sing. **Travel Song**

I'm with _____,
And you're with _____,
We're together in a boat on the blue, blue sea.

She's with _____,
And he's with _____,
They're together in a helicopter.

We're with _____,
And you're with _____,
We're together on a yellow school bus.

WORKBOOK page 25

GRAMMAR GUIDE page 130

Lesson 7

FACTUAL READER

LET'S VISIT MALAYSIA

1 Read about a special festival in Malaysia.

Mail

Dear Pen Pal,

My name's Pao-Pei. I'm nine years old, and I live in Pasir-Gudang, in Malaysia. I want to tell you about a special festival in my hometown. Every year we have an international kite festival in February. Kites are very popular in Malaysia. Are they popular in your country? People from all over the world, including Germany, the USA, and Taiwan, visit us for our colorful festival. The kites are fantastic; they're beautiful.

Please tell me about a festival in your country.

Write me soon,

Pao-Pei

It's a fact!

Kite flying is a very old tradition in Asia – it's more than 2,300 years old!

2 Read and answer.

1 What is Pao-Pei's nationality?

2 Find words she uses to describe the festival and the kites.

3 Can you describe the kite in the picture?

Think Twice

1 Compare the kite festival to a festival in your country. How is it the same or different?

2 How do festivals help you to understand other people?

Lesson 8

SPEAKING TIME

PRESENTATION: A FESTIVAL IN YOUR COUNTRY

1. Prepare.

Find information about the festival.
Use the questions below to help you.

- Choose a festival from your country.
- Draw a picture and label it.
- Find information about it.

- When is the festival?
- What clothes do people wear?
- What is the festival called?
- What happens at the festival?
- Why do you like it?

2. Practice.

Describe your festival.

- Let me tell you about …
- The festival is in …
- People wear …
- I like the festival because …

3. Present.

Let me tell you about our Halloween festival. It's cool. The festival is in October – the thirty-first – and it's really spooky. People wear scary costumes like ghosts or witches. And they make faces in pumpkins. I like the festival because we play tricks on people.

WORKBOOK page 26

41

ITALY

UNIT 4

We're in Venice, Italy! Let's go explore!

Here we go!

This is a river taxi in Venice. It's called a gondola.

What do you know about Italy?
Can you name some famous food from Italy?
What types of transportation do people use in your country?

ZOOM IN

Look at the picture.
How are the people in the picture traveling? Why?

Lesson 1

·VOCABULARY·

TRACK 30

1 Listen, point, and say.

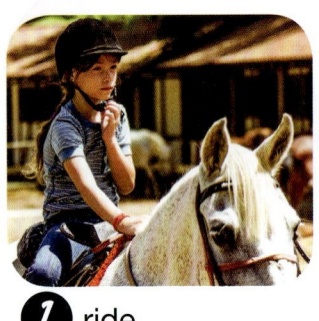

1 ride
2 dive 
3 climb 
4 ski 
5 surf 
6 fish 
7 skate 
8 skateboard 

2 Circle the correct option.

1 You can   surf / ride horses   in the ocean.
2 You can   fish / dive   in a pool.
3 You can   ski / skateboard   in the mountains.
4 You can   skate / climb   in the mountains.

3 Check your answers with a friend.

Can you skateboard in the ocean?

No, I can't.

WORKBOOK
page 27

44

Lesson 2

1 Listen, read, and say.

GRAMMAR
I'm fish**ing**. **I'm not** swimm**ing**.
We're sail**ing**. **We aren't** walk**ing**.

Zac and Oona are in Italy.

Look! We're sailing in a boat. We aren't swimming.

And I'm fishing, too!

DISCOVER GRAMMAR

Circle.
To say what is happening now, we use:
I'm + **climb** / **climbing**.
We aren't + **ride** / **riding**.

2 Write sentences.

I _____ riding a horse.

I _____ surfing.

We _____ fishing.

We _____ climbing.

3 Act it out. Then say.

We're walking.

WORKBOOK page 28

GRAMMAR GUIDE page 130

Lesson 3 — SOUNDS AND SPELLING

sk **sw** **str**

TRACK 32

1 Listen and chant.

Skyler is strong. What can she do?
She can swim and skate very well,
And she can ski, too!

Skyler is hungry. What can she eat?
Strawberries and cream,
And something very sweet!

2 Circle, sort, and write.

strongswimstrawberryskatesweetski

sk	sw	str
_____	_____	_____
_____	_____	_____

3 Write a word with *sk*, *sw*, or *str*.

❶ _____

❷ _____

❸ _____

46

Lesson 4 · READING TIME ·

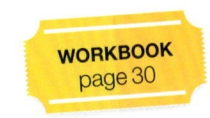

TRACK 33

1 Listen and read.

1 Some children like skating.
- Here, let's skate together.
- Oops!

2 Some children like swimming in the ocean.
- Come and swim with us!

3 Some children like bowling.
- Strike!
- She's strong!
- Hey! It's my turn.

4 Everyone likes having friends.
- Goal!

2 Read the story again. Check (✓) the **value**.

Solidarity: Play together. ○   Play with your best friend. ○

3 Read and check (✓).

How do you feel when you are not in the game?   ✓ ○   ✗ ○

What can you do if someone is alone?

Invite him / her to watch your game. ○   Invite him / her to play with you. ○

WORKBOOK page 30

Lesson 5

VOCABULARY

TRACK 34

1 Listen, point, and say.

1. ping pong
2. tennis
3. baseball
4. soccer
5. ice hockey
6. basketball

TRACK 35

2 Listen and guess the sports.

3 Talk to a friend.

> I like basketball. I don't like tennis.

TRACK 36

4 Listen and complete. Then sing. **Cool Sports**

We're smart and we play sports,
We're strong and we're athletic,
We're cool, so cool!
We're playing _____.

We're smart and we play sports,
We're strong and we're athletic,
We're cool, so cool!
_____.

We're smart and we play sports,
We're strong and we're athletic,
We're cool, so cool!
_____.

WORKBOOK page 31

48

Lesson 6

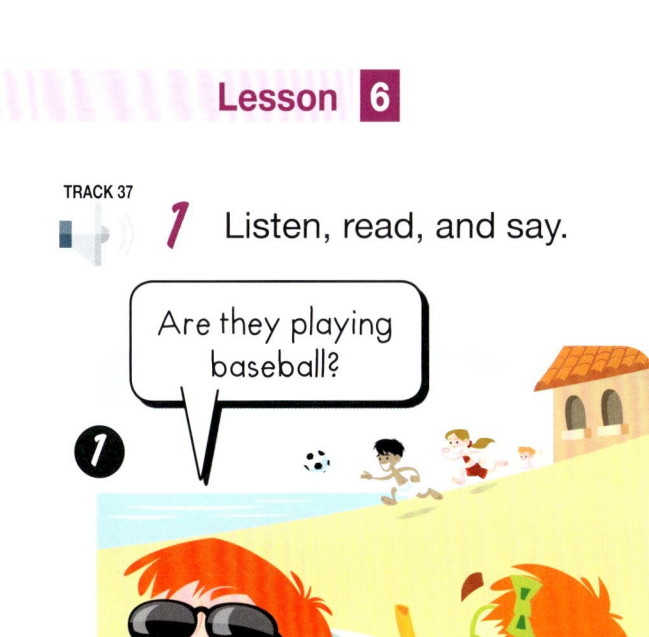

GRAMMAR

Are you / they swimming?
Yes, **I am**. / No, **I'm not**.
Yes, **they are**. / No, **they aren't**.

TRACK 37

1 Listen, read, and say.

1. Are they playing baseball?

   No, they aren't. They're playing soccer. Look!

2. Are you eating ice cream?

   Yes, I am.

DISCOVER GRAMMAR

Circle.

To ask a question, we use:

Are you playing? / You are playing?

They are skating? / Are they skating?

2 Look at Activity 1. Write *No, they aren't* or *Yes, they are*.

1 Are Zac and Oona swimming? _____.

2 Are the children playing soccer? _____.

3 Are they playing basketball? _____.

3 Choose a sport. Play the Guessing Game.

Are you playing baseball?

Yes, I am.

WORKBOOK page 32

GRAMMAR GUIDE page 130

49

Lesson 7

FACTUAL READER

LET'S VISIT ITALY

1 Read about soccer camps in Italy.

Future stars
by Anna Totti

Meet Giovanna Neri, a typical 9-year-old girl from Milan, Italy. Like many children in Italy, Giovanna is crazy about soccer. Her favorite team is AC Milan. Right now she is at a summer soccer camp in a town called Jesolo. Jesolo is a beautiful place by the ocean. Lots of people are at the beach sailing, swimming, and surfing. Giovanna is meeting new friends at soccer camp and having a lot of fun. The most important part of soccer camp is learning to respect your companions and learning new skills.

2 Read and answer.

1 What is Giovanna doing this summer?
2 What do you know about Jesolo?
3 Is this article positive or negative about soccer camps?

It's a fact!
The Azzurri are the national soccer team of Italy. Azzurri means "the blues" – it's the color of their uniform!

Think Twice
1 Do you like learning new skills? Why / Why not?
2 Why do you think sports camps are important?

Lesson 8

SPEAKING TIME

PRESENTATION — A POPULAR SPORT IN YOUR COUNTRY

1. Prepare.

Find information about the sport. Use the questions below to help you.

- Choose a popular sport from your country.
- Draw a picture and label it.
- Find information about it.

- Is it a team sport or an individual sport?
- Is there a national team?
- How many players are there?
- What are they called and why?
- What equipment do they use?
- Why do you like this sport?

2. Practice.

Describe the popular sport in your country.

- Let me tell you about …
- The national team is …
- The players wear …
- They play with …
- There are … players on a team.
- I like this sport because …

TRACK 38

3. Present.

Hi, I'm Liam from New Zealand. Let me tell you about our national sport – it's rugby, and it's really popular. The national team is the All Blacks because they wear black shirts and shorts. They play with an oval-shaped ball. There are 15 players on the team. I like this sport because it's fun to watch.

Rugby

WORKBOOK page 33

PROGRESS CHECK

1 Unscramble, then write. /5

1 aimasayl — Malaysia — He's Malaysian.
2 ketyur — _____ — _____.
3 het sua — _____ — _____.
4 comiex — _____ — _____.
5 pajan — _____ — _____.
6 asnip — _____ — _____.

2 Complete using words from the box. /5

| ~~me~~ us him her it them |

1 I can see Zac. He's waving to ___me___.
2 Where's your sister? I can't see _____.
3 There are some cherries. Can you pass _____ to me, please?
4 From up here we can see our friends, but they can't see _____.
5 I love chocolate. Do you like _____, too?
6 Paul is my brother. Do you know _____?

TOTAL /10

PROGRESS CHECK

1 Choose and check (✓) four activities. Then answer *Yes, I am* or *No, I'm not*. /5

eating chocolate ◯
watching TV ◯
playing a computer game ◯
riding an elephant ◯
playing ping pong ✓
skating ◯

1 Are you playing ping pong? <u>Yes, I am</u>.
2 Are you playing a computer game? _____.
3 Are you eating chocolate? _____.
4 Are you watching TV? _____.
5 Are you skating? _____.
6 Are you riding an elephant? _____.

2 Read and complete. /5

Hello, Oliver!

I'm on vacation in Italy, and I'm having fun. Today **1** I <u>'m</u> <u>swimming</u> in the ocean and **2** I _____ _____ soccer on the beach with my brother. **3** We _____ _____ a kite today. My friends are here, too. **4** They _____ _____ ice cream, but I don't like strawberry, so **5** I _____ not _____ my ice cream.

Now I'm watching two boys. **6** They _____ _____.

It's a great vacation!

Bye, Vicky

TOTAL /10

WORKBOOK page 35   **STICKERS**   **PASSPORT** page 8

53

MALAYSIA

The Petronas Twin Towers in Kuala Lumpur.

The towers are 88 stories tall (451.9 meters).

The Twin Towers built: 1994-1996.

STEAM

TEAM NAME

What is a tower?

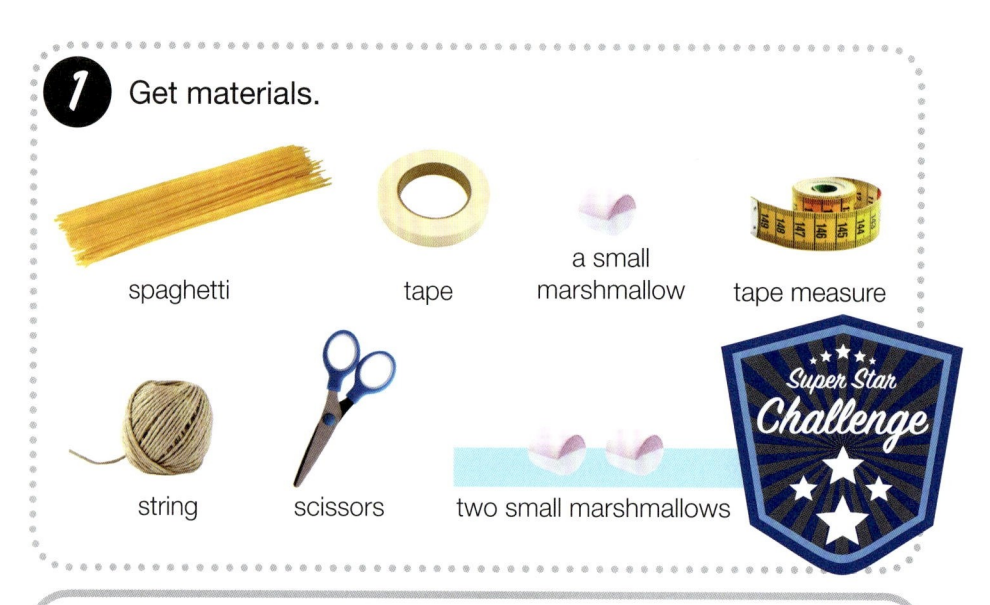

1 Get materials.

- spaghetti
- tape
- a small marshmallow
- tape measure
- string
- scissors
- two small marshmallows

Super Star Challenge

There is a bridge 41-42 stories up. It stabilizes the movement of the Petronas Twin Towers when it's windy.

There are 7 bells at the top of the Tower of Pisa. One bell for each note of the musical major scale.

54

CHALLENGE 2

· BUILD A TOWER ·

ITALY

2 Build the tallest tower with your kit!

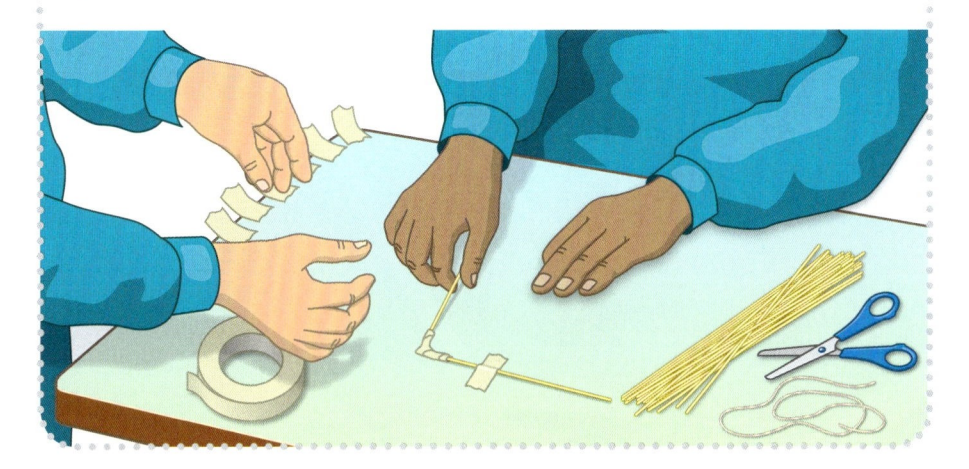

The Leaning Tower of Pisa is the bell tower next to the cathedral.

3 The marshmallow must stay on top.

4 Measure your tower. How tall is it?
_____

The tower is 8 stories tall (original height 60 meters/current height 56.67-55.86 meters).

5 Draw your tower.

6 Draw a new design.

Super Star Challenge
Try again. Go higher! Add 2 marshmallows.

What do you like and dislike about your team's design?

The Tower of Pisa built: 1173-1372.

TEAMWORK ★★★★☆

55

JAMAICA

UNIT 5

Jamaica is beautiful!

Jamaica is a hot and sunny island with beautiful beaches.

Is Jamaica in the Caribbean or in Africa?
What language do they speak in Jamaica?
What is typical weather for your country?

Look at the picture.
Do you think fishing is this man's hobby?

Lesson 1 · VOCABULARY·

TRACK 39

1 Listen, point, and say.

❶	❷	❸	❹	❺	❻	❼
Sunday	Monday	Tuesday	Wednesday	Thursday	Friday	Saturday
sunny	cloudy	foggy	windy	hot	cold snowy	rainy

2 Write and say.

1 It isn't _____windy_____.
It's _____sunny_____.
Let's go skateboarding in the park.

2 It isn't _____.
It's _____.
Let's go swimming in the ocean.

3 It isn't _____.
It's _____.
Let's go skiing in the mountains.

4 It isn't _____.
It's _____.
Let's go fishing in the river.

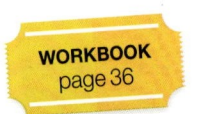

WORKBOOK page 36

Lesson 2

GRAMMAR

What's he / she / it **doing?**
He's / She's / It's sleep**ing**.
He / She / It isn't read**ing**.

TRACK 40

1 Listen, read, and say.

It's hot. Zac isn't playing soccer. He's playing his guitar. Oona isn't reading her book. She's sleeping under a tree.

Look at the bird! It's singing. It likes Zac's song.

DISCOVER GRAMMAR

Circle.
What **is she / she is** doing?
She's / Is she sleeping.
Isn't she / She isn't swimming.

TRACK 41

2 Listen and say *True* or *False*.

3 Choose and circle. Then say.

Look at Zac. What's he doing?

1 **He's / He isn't** sleeping.   2 **He's / He isn't** playing his guitar.

Look at Oona. What's she doing?

3 **She's / She isn't** sleeping.   4 **She's / She isn't** reading.

Look at the bird. What's it doing?

5 **It's / It isn't** flying.   6 **It's / It isn't** singing.

WORKBOOK page 37   GRAMMAR GUIDE page 131

Lesson 3

SOUNDS AND SPELLING

oo **ir** **ow**

TRACK 42

1 Listen and chant.

Off to school! Where's my shirt?
And my socks, and boots, and skirt?

Off to the country! Look, a cow!
Flowers and trees and a big brown owl.

Off to the pool! It's really cool!
It's sunny today — I'm not going to school!

TRACK 43

2 Listen and complete. Then cross (✗) out the word with a different sound.

1 c ___ ___ l
   sch ___ ___ l
   fl _o_ _w_ er
   _____

2 sh ___ ___ t
   c ___ ___ l
   sk ___ ___ t
   _____

3 fl ___ ___ er
   ___ ___ l
   sh ___ ___ t
   _____

3 Look at the pictures. Find one more word for each column.

Lesson 4 # READING TIME

TRACK 44

1 Listen and read.

1 Kirsty is walking to school. She's wearing her skirt and her shirt, but she doesn't have her sweater.

I'm cold! I don't have my sweater.

2 It's rainy. Kirsty is playing in the flowers in the park. She's wearing her new shoes.

Oh, no! My new shoes! I don't have my boots.

3 Kirsty is at the pool. She has her sweater, her new shoes, her brown boots …

4 … but she can't go swimming.

Oh, no! I don't have my bathing suit!

2 Read the story again. Check (✓) the **value**.

Responsibility: Be prepared. ◯   Be kind. ◯

3 Are you prepared and organized? Read and write *Yes* or *No*.

I make lists to help me remember. _____

I keep my bedroom neat. _____

I organize my school bag every day. _____

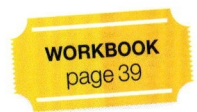

WORKBOOK page 39

Lesson 5 · VOCABULARY·

TRACK 45

1 Listen, point, and say.

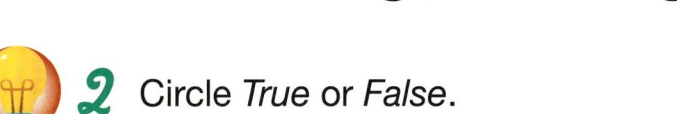

1 dress
2 shorts 
3 T-shirt 
4 jeans  
5 socks 
6 boots 

2 Circle *True* or *False*.

1 Rosa's wearing socks.   True / False
2 She's wearing boots.   True / False
3 Rosa's wearing a dress.   True / False
4 Ben's wearing a T-shirt.   True / False
5 Ben's wearing jeans.   True / False
6 He's wearing shorts.   True / False

Rosa   Ben

3 Talk to a friend about Rosa and Ben.

Rosa's wearing a T-shirt.

No, she's wearing a dress.

4 Choose a picture and play the Guessing Game. Listen and point.

She's wearing a red skirt.

WORKBOOK
page 40

Lesson 6

GRAMMAR

Is he / she read**ing**?
Yes, **he / she is**.
No, **he / she isn't**.

TRACK 46

1 Listen, read, and say.

Zac and Oona are at the train station. They're looking for Zac's friend Paul.

PLATFORM #3

Look! There's my friend.

Where? Is he wearing a hat?

No, he isn't.

Is he reading a book?

Yes, he is. Hello, Paul!

DISCOVER GRAMMAR

Circle the correct answers.
Is he riding a bike?

Yes, he is.   A bike.   He's riding a bike.   No, he isn't.

2 Unscramble the questions, and answer them.

1 wearing Paul Is a hat? <u>Is Paul wearing a hat</u>_____.

2 Oona a banana? Is eating _____.

3 Paul a book? reading Is _____.

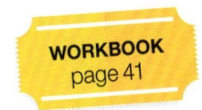

TRACK 47

3 Listen and complete. Then sing. **The Island Song**

It's a sunny afternoon,
On an island in the sun.
What's he doing?
He's having fun!

What's she doing?
Is she _____ a kite?
No, she isn't.
She's _____ a bike!

WORKBOOK page 41

GRAMMAR GUIDE page 131

63

Lesson 7

FACTUAL READER

LET'S VISIT JAMAICA

1 Read a poem about Jamaica.

Jamaica's Weather
by Winston Miller

Jamaica's weather,
Is great for us all!
Jamaica's weather,
Is great for us all!

It's hot and it's sunny,
And sometimes it rains.
It can be very windy,
Watch out for hurricanes!

It's hot on the beach,
But it's fresh in the pool,
And up in the mountains,
It can be a little cool!

Jamaica's weather,
Is great for us all!
Jamaica's weather,
Is great for us all!

It's a fact!
The gold color in the Jamaican flag represents the beautiful sunny weather in Jamaica.

2 Read and write.

1 Find seven weather words in the poem.

2 What's the weather like in a hurricane?

3 Does the poet like the weather in Jamaica?

Think Twice

1 Is the weather in Jamaica great for everybody all the time? Why? Why not?

2 Think about the weather patterns in your country.
Are there any problems because of the weather?

Lesson 8

SPEAKING TIME

PRESENTATION — THE WEATHER IN YOUR COUNTRY

TEMPLATE 5

1 Prepare.

Find information about the weather. Use the questions below to help you.

- Think about the weather in your country in the different seasons.
- Draw a picture and label it.
- Find information about temperatures and weather patterns.

What is the temperature?

Is the weather the same in different parts of your country?

What is the weather like?

Do you like this time of year? Why?

2 Practice.

Describe the weather in your country.

Let me tell you about …

It's great / hot and sunny …

In the winter / summer …

TRACK 48

3 Present.

Let me tell you about the weather in Florida. It's really great. It's usually hot and sunny, especially in spring and summer. In winter it's warm, too. But the weather isn't always great. In the hurricane season sometimes it can be really windy and stormy.

WORKBOOK page 42

CHILE

COMODORO ARTURO MERINO BENÍTEZ INTERNATIONAL AIRPORT

Welcome to Chile! Look at his horse!

UNIT 6

This man lives on a farm in Chile. He's going to ride his horse to the mountains.

Is Chile near your country?
Is Chile a big country or a small country?
Can you ride a horse?

Look at the picture.
What is the weather like?

Lesson 1 · VOCABULARY ·

TRACK 49

1 Listen, point, and say.

1. hospital
2. café 
3. supermarket 
4. library 
5. museum 
6. movie theater 
7. airport 
8. farm 

2 Look and write.

1 She's at the _____.
2 He's at the _____.
3 She's at the _____.
4 They're at the _____.
5 They're at the _____.
6 He's at the _____.

3 Ask and answer.

Is there a supermarket in your neighborhood?

Yes, there is. Is there a museum in your neighborhood?

WORKBOOK page 43

68

Lesson 2

TRACK 50

1 Listen, read, and say.

GRAMMAR

Are you / we going to the movie theater?
Yes, **I am / we are**.
No, **I'm not / we aren't**.

It's 8 o'clock. Zac and Oona are going to the movie theater.

Are you going to the movie theater?

No, we aren't. We're going to the stadium. There's a music festival.

Now I'm going to the stadium, too!

DISCOVER GRAMMAR

Circle the correct alternatives.
Are **I / you / he / she / it / we / they** going to the park?

2 Complete the sentences.

1
We _____ the library.
We _____ the pool.

2
They _____ the supermarket.
They _____ the airport.

3 Think of a place. Ask and answer.

Are you going to the pool?

No, I'm not. I'm going to the museum.

WORKBOOK page 44

GRAMMAR GUIDE page 131

69

Lesson 3

SOUNDS AND SPELLING

TRACK 51

1 Listen to the poem.

er　ear　ore

I'm playing with my brother.
We're very, very bored.
Let's go down to the river.
Let's go off and explore!

We're going to the river.
The water's really cool!
More fun than the teacher
And boring stuff in school.

Now we're going to eat
Some chocolate and a pear.
An animal is watching us.
Look! A hungry bear!

2 Find the words in the puzzle. Then write.

r	t	e	a	c	h	e	r	p	w
i	b	e	a	r	h	w	k	e	a
v	e	x	p	l	o	r	e	a	t
w	q	b	r	o	t	h	e	r	e
r	b	o	r	e	d	h	r	l	r

er
_____
_____
_____
_____

ear
_____
_____
_____

ore
_____
_____
_____

3 Write one more word for each column.

WORKBOOK page 45

70

Lesson 4 # READING TIME

TRACK 52

1 Listen and read.

1.
- I'm bored. Are you going to the river?
- Yes, I am. Can you swim?
- Yes, I can.

2.
- Look! There's a bear. Let's be careful.
- Oh, I see bears all the time.

3.
- Mmm, these pears are delicious.
- A bear! Quick! Jump!

4.
- Help! I can't swim!

5.
- I hate the water!

2 Read the story again. Check (✓) the **value**.

Honesty: Always be careful. ◯   Don't pretend. ◯

3 Are you always honest? Read and write *Yes* or *No*.

1 I say what I can and can't do. _____

2 I tell the truth to my friends. _____

3 I am always honest with my parents. _____

WORKBOOK page 46

Lesson 5

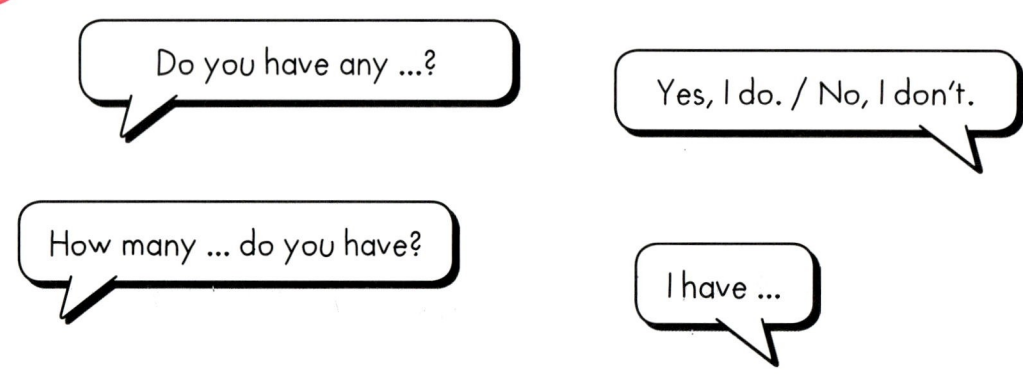

VOCABULARY

TRACK 53

1 Listen, point, and say.

I'm Ken. This is my family.

1. uncle
2. aunt
3. cousin
4. baby sister
5. baby brother
6. grandparents

TRACK 54

2 Look at Activity 1. Listen and say the person.

3 Talk to a friend about their family.

- Do you have any ...?
- Yes, I do. / No, I don't.
- How many ... do you have?
- I have ...

WORKBOOK page 47

Lesson 6

1 Listen, read, and say. (TRACK 55)

GRAMMAR

Where's he / she **going**?
He's / She's going to the airport.
Is he / she **going to** the beach?
Yes, **he / she is**. / No, **he / she isn't**.

Where's Zac going? He's going to the airport with his grandparents.

And Oona is going to the airport, too!

DISCOVER GRAMMAR

Read again. Circle.

The story is talking about **now** / **the future**.

2 Complete the questions using *Where are* or *Where's*. Then answer.

1 _____ Zac going? _____.
2 _____ Oona going? _____.
3 _____ Zac's grandparents going? _____.

3 Listen, sing, and act. **The Busy, Busy Song** (TRACK 56)

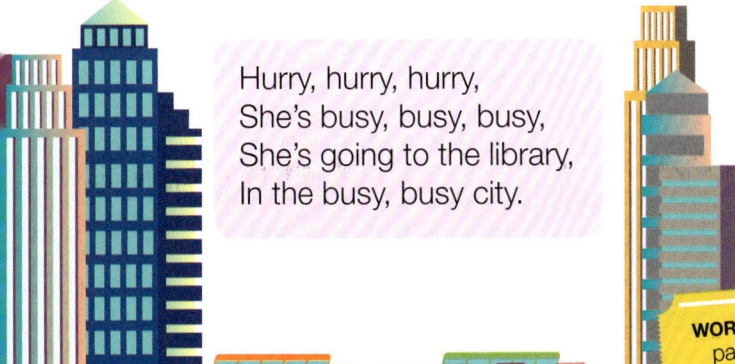

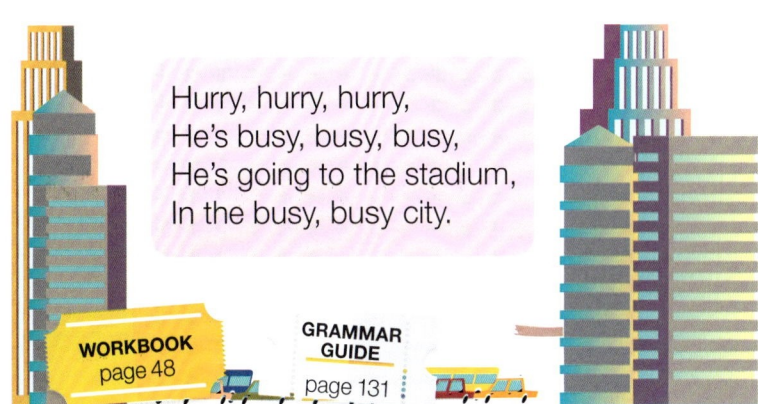

Hurry, hurry, hurry,
She's busy, busy, busy,
She's going to the library,
In the busy, busy city.

Hurry, hurry, hurry,
He's busy, busy, busy,
He's going to the stadium,
In the busy, busy city.

WORKBOOK page 48

GRAMMAR GUIDE page 131

Lesson 7

·FACTUAL READER·

LET'S VISIT CHILE

1. Read about a famous glacier in Chile.

www.kidsonvacation.com

Where can you go skiing in July, swim in the ocean on Christmas Day, see penguins and llamas, and eat German desserts? In Chile, of course. This long, skinny country is a very special place with many interesting places to visit.

One fantastic place is the Grey Glacier on Lake Grey in the south of Chile. Glaciers are large, frozen rivers that are usually covered in snow. They are very beautiful. Lake Grey also has icebergs! You can visit the Grey Glacier by boat, and you can also go ice walking!

It's a fact!

Almost 90 percent of an iceberg is under water!

2. Read and write.

1. What types of animals live in Chile?
2. What are glaciers made of?
3. What can you do at the glacier?

Think Twice

1. Do you think the Grey Glacier is a good place for a vacation? Why / Why not?
2. Do you know any other vacation places that are unusual?

Lesson 8 — SPEAKING TIME

PRESENTATION: A SPECIAL PLACE IN YOUR COUNTRY

1 Prepare.

Find information about the place. Use the questions below to help you.

- Choose a special place of natural beauty in your country.
- Draw a picture and label it.
- Find information about the place.

Why is it special?

What can you do there?

Why do you like it?

2 Practice.

Describe your special place.

Let me tell you about …

You can …

I like … because …

TRACK 57

3 Present.

Let me tell you about the Grand Canyon. You can travel down there on a horse, or you can fly over in a plane. You can see different birds and animals there. I like it because it's really interesting.

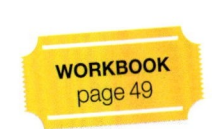

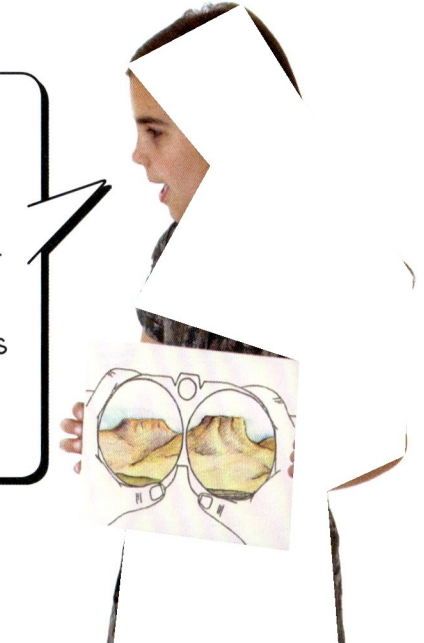

WORKBOOK page 49

PROGRESS CHECK

1 Unscramble the verbs. Complete the sentences. Then number the pictures. /5

1	ngis	_sing_	He's _singing_ a song.
2	kirdn	_____	She's _____ some soda.
3	epels	_____	The dog's _____ under the table.
4	iatpn	_____	He's _____ a picture.
5	ocok	_____	She's _____ some spaghetti.
6	tae	_____	The cat's _____ some ice cream.

2 Look and answer. /5

1 Is Zac playing soccer? _Yes, he is_ .
2 Is Oona reading a book? _____ .
3 Is the sun shining? _____ .
4 What is the bird doing in the tree? _____ .
5 What is the boy doing in the ocean? _____ .
6 What are the two girls doing? _____ .

TOTAL /10

WORKBOOK page 50   STICKERS   PASSPORT page 10

PROGRESS CHECK

1 Choose and check (✓) four places. Then answer *Yes, I am* or *No, I'm not.* /5

- the café ○
- the mall ✓
- the movie theater ○
- the library ○
- the pool ○
- the country ○

1 Are you going to the mall? <u>Yes, I am</u>.
2 Are you going to the movie theater? _____.
3 Are you going to the café? _____.
4 Are you going to the pool? _____.
5 Are you going to the country? _____.
6 Are you going to the library? _____.

2 Look at the picture. Answer the questions. /5

1 LIBRARY **2** CAFÉ **3** SUPERMARKET **4** HOSPITAL **5** MOVIE THEATER **6** MUSEUM

1 Where's the boy going? <u>He's going to the library</u>.
2 Is the girl going to the library? _____.
3 Where's the woman going? _____.
4 Are the doctors going to the hospital? _____.
5 Where are the two girls going? _____.
6 Where are the children going? _____.

TOTAL /10

WORKBOOK page 51 STICKERS PASSPORT page 12

JAMAICA

Jamaica is one of 700 Caribbean islands.

Jamaica is an island, but the country of Jamaica has 28 other islands!

Jamaica has mountains, rainforests, and beaches.

2.9 million people live in Jamaica.

STEAM

TEAM NAME

Can you find Jamaica or Chile on a world map?

1 Get materials.

- salt
- water
- white glue
- paper plate
- flour
- gouache paint
- paintbrushes
- cardstock paper
- colored pencils

Super Star Challenge

2 Prepare the salt dough.

EASTER ISLAND (RAPA NUI)

This physical map shows the land, the coast, and the sea around Rapa Nui.

This digital relief map shows the physical features of Jamaica.

78

CHALLENGE 3

· CREATE AN ISLAND ·

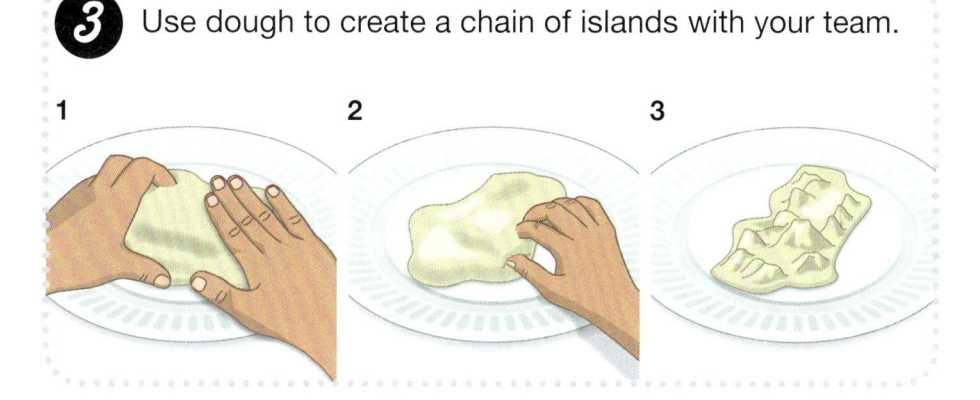

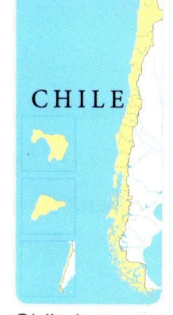

CHILE

3 Use dough to create a chain of islands with your team.

1 2 3

Chile has over 5000 islands.

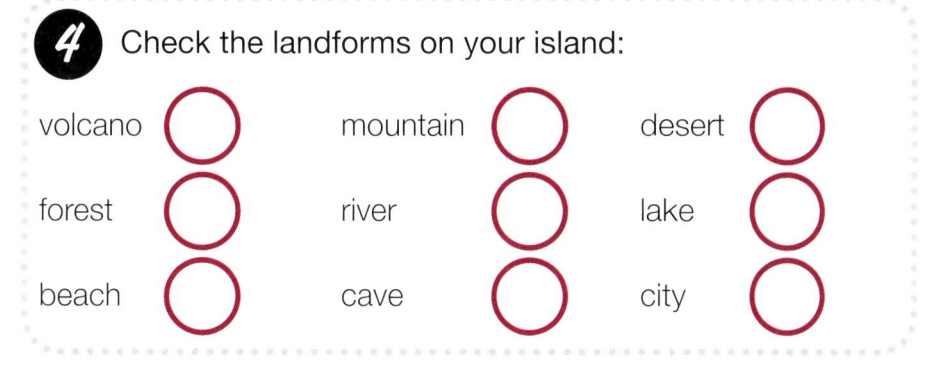

4 Check the landforms on your island:

- volcano ○
- mountain ○
- desert ○
- forest ○
- river ○
- lake ○
- beach ○
- cave ○
- city ○

Rapa Nui has 887 Moai.

5 Let the dough dry and paint.

There are 3 volcanoes on Rapa Nui.

How can you represent the 3D features of your island on a 2D map?

Super Star Challenge
Create a postcard for your island.

Chile has 18 million inhabitants.

TEAMWORK ★★★★☆

79

FRANCE

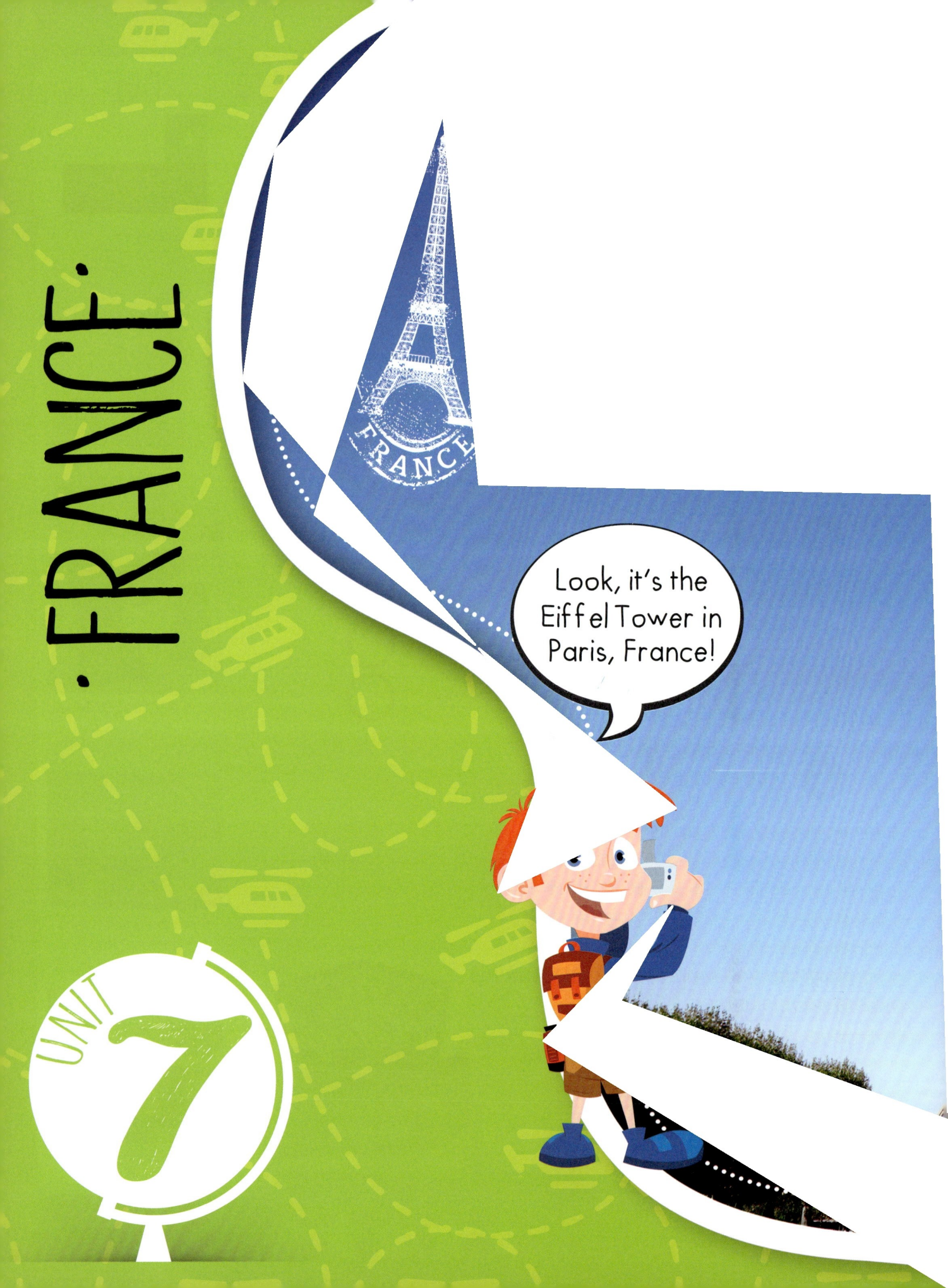

Unit 7

Look, it's the Eiffel Tower in Paris, France!

About six million people visit the Eiffel Tower every year.

Paris is the capital of France.
What do you know about it?
What language do people speak in France?
Is there a big tower in your country? Can you climb it?

Look at the picture.
Imagine you are at the top of the Eiffel Tower.
What do you think you can see?

ZOOM IN

UNIT 7

Lesson 1

VOCABULARY

TRACK 58

1 Listen, point, and say.

1 fisherman **3** pilot **5** wrestler **7** firefighter
2 nurse **4** writer **6** vet **8** police officer

2 Read and complete.

1 He likes flying. He works in an airport. He's a _____pilot_____.

2 She likes writing. She likes books. She's a _____.

3 He's athletic and very strong. He works in a stadium. He's a _____.

4 She works in a hospital. She's a _____.

5 He likes the ocean. He works on a boat. He's a _____.

6 She likes animals. She works in an animal hospital. She's a _____.

7 He's brave and he helps people. He's a _____.

8 She wears a uniform. She works with people and she is very responsible. She's a _____.

3 Play the Guessing Game. Then spell.

He's a wrestler.

WORKBOOK page 52

Lesson 2

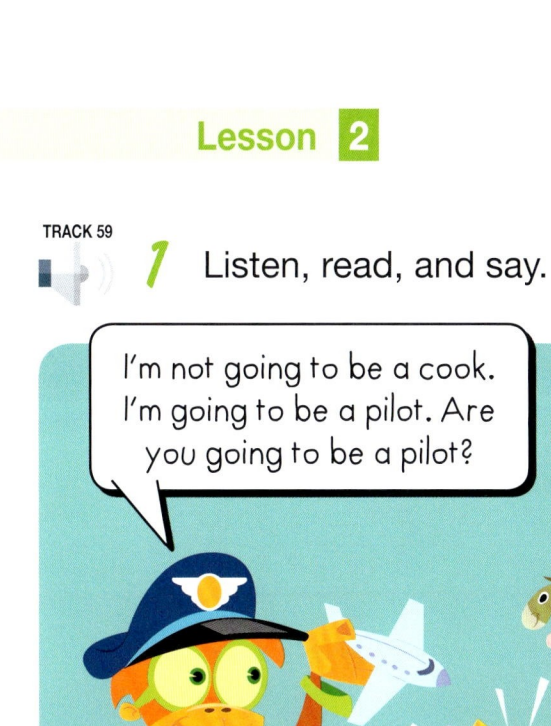

GRAMMAR

I'm (not) going to be a cook.
Are you going to be a pilot?
Yes, I am. / No, I'm not.

TRACK 59

1 Listen, read, and say.

I'm not going to be a cook. I'm going to be a pilot. Are you going to be a pilot?

No, I'm not.

I'm going to be a vet.

DISCOVER GRAMMAR

Match.

To talk about now, we use: I'm going to be a vet.
To talk about a future plan, we use: I am a vet.

2 Write two sentences about yourself. Then talk to a friend.

police officer   firefighter   nurse   vet   teacher
farmer   fisherman   wrestler   pilot   writer

1 I'm _____.

2 I'm not _____.

Are you going to be a fisherman?

No, I'm not. I'm going to be a ...

WORKBOOK page 53   GRAMMAR GUIDE page 132

83

Lesson 3 · SOUNDS AND SPELLING·

ur | or | a

TRACK 60

1 Listen to the poem.

Dogs, cats, and turtles!
My father is a vet.
He works in a world of animals,
With all kinds of pets.

My mother is a nurse.
She drives a purple car.
She works at the hospital.
It isn't very far.

I'm going to be a writer
And work with lots of words.
I'm going to write poems
About surfing, fish, and birds.

TRACK 61

2 Listen and complete. Then cross (X) out the word with a different sound.

1 f __ ther   2 c __ r   3 n __ __ se
   n _u_ _r_ se   w __ __ k   t __ __ tle
   c __ r   w __ __ ld   f __ ther

   _____   _____   _____

3 Look back at the poem. Find one more word for each column.

WORKBOOK page 54

Lesson 4

·READING TIME·

TRACK 62

1 Listen and read.

1
Look at the firefighters.
What a great job! I'm going to be a firefighter.
It's a lot of work.

2
Look at the police officer in his fast car.
It's a lot of work.
What a great job! I'm going to be a police officer.

3
Look at the nurse helping the old man.
It's a lot of work.
What a great job! I'm going to be a nurse.

4
Dad is right. This *is* a lot of work!

2 Read the story again. Check (✓) the *value*.

Effort: Do your homework. ○   Work hard. ○

3 Do you always work hard? Read and check (✓) what you do.

1 I always try hard at school. ○

2 I never miss a class. ○

3 I do my homework regularly. ○

WORKBOOK page 55

Unit 7 · Lesson 5 · VOCABULARY

TRACK 63

1 Listen, point, and say.

1. do my homework
2. take a shower 
3. call a friend 
4. use the Internet 
5. brush my teeth 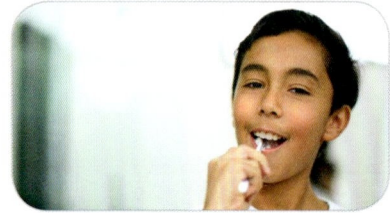
6. buy candy 

2 Look at Activity 1. Write true sentences in your notebook. Then talk to a friend.

> I brush my teeth every day. I don't use the Internet every day.

TRACK 64

3 Listen and sing. **School Days**

Monday through Friday,
Before I go to school,
I get ready in the bathroom,
What do you think I do?

Take a shower! Brush your teeth
and comb your hair!

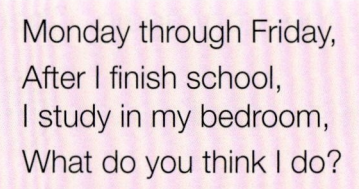

Monday through Friday,
After I finish school,
I study in my bedroom,
What do you think I do?

Do your homework! Call a friend
and use the Internet!

WORKBOOK page 56

Lesson 6

GRAMMAR

He's / She's going to take a shower.
He / She isn't going to watch TV.
Is he / she going to play soccer?
Yes, **he / she is**. / No, **he / she isn't**.

TRACK 65

1 Listen, read, and say.

Oona's going to brush her teeth. She isn't going to take a shower.

Zac's going to take a shower.

Oops!

DISCOVER GRAMMAR

Circle the possible alternatives.
She **is / are / isn't / aren't** going to have dinner.

2 Make sentences. Then answer the questions.

1 Zac / brush / ? / teeth _____
2 Zac / ? / take a shower _____
3 Oona / ? / brush / teeth _____
4 Oona / take a shower / ? _____

3 Talk to a friend about what you are going to do after school today. Then tell the class.

watch TV   play soccer   make a model
play a computer game
listen to music   read a book

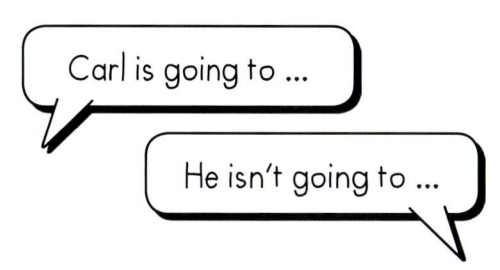

Carl is going to ...

He isn't going to ...

WORKBOOK page 57   GRAMMAR GUIDE page 132

Lesson 7

FACTUAL READER

LET'S VISIT FRANCE

1 Read about ski schools for children in France.

Vacations in the snow

In France, skiing is very popular. In some ski resorts, there are ski schools for children. They start learning how to ski in special places called "snow gardens." They learn by playing a lot of games and having fun.

Claude Lechaume is a ski instructor. In winter, Claude works at a ski resort near a big mountain in France, called Mont Blanc. For the rest of the year, he works as a writer. The children at the ski school love Claude's lessons, and they love Claude.

It's a fact!

Children of three years of age can go to ski school in France!

It's important for children to feel happy on their skis and happy on the snow.

I'm going to be a writer!

I'm going to be a ski instructor!

2 Find and write.

1 How do children learn to ski?

2 How many jobs does Claude have?

Think Twice

1 Why do you think Claude's students love him?

2 Which of Claude's jobs do you think is more difficult? Why?

Lesson 8 — SPEAKING TIME

PRESENTATION: A TEACHER OR INSTRUCTOR YOU ADMIRE

1. Prepare.

Find information about the person. Use the questions below to help you.

- Choose a special person to talk about.
- Draw or glue pictures of him / her, and add labels.
- Find information about him / her.

What does he / she teach?

Where does he / she work?

What special activities does he / she do?

Who are his / her students?

Why do you admire this teacher / instructor?

2. Practice.

Describe your special person.

- Let me tell you about …
- He / She works …
- His / Her lessons are …
- His / Her students are …
- I admire him / her because …

TRACK 66

3. Present.

Let me tell you about my soccer coach. His name is Rick. He works at the community center, and his lessons are great. We all want to learn his soccer skills. I admire him because he is a good teacher and he's a fantastic soccer player.

WORKBOOK page 58

USA

Unit 8

"We're in the USA. It's Independence Day."

I'm Lucy Hill, and I was born in the USA.

Independence Day is on the fourth of July.

What is the capital city of the USA?
Do you know how many states there are? How many can you name?
Do you have parades in your country? When?

Look at the picture. What is happening in Lucy's city today?

Lesson 1 VOCABULARY

TRACK 67

1 Listen, point, and say. Then ask and answer.

1. January	2. February	3. March
4. April	5. May	6. June
7. July Oona's Birthday	8. August	9. September
10. October	11. November	12. December

When's your birthday?

My birthday's in July.

TRACK 68

2 Listen and say what's next.

3 Find out and complete the birthday chart.

1 When's your teacher's birthday?
2 When's your best friend's birthday?
3 When's your mom's birthday?
4 When's your birthday?

WORKBOOK page 59

92

Lesson 2

GRAMMAR

I was / They were born in a hospital / March.
Were you born in January?
Yes, **I was.** / No, **I wasn't.**
Were they born in June?
Yes, **they were.** / No, **they weren't.**

TRACK 69

1 Listen, read, and say.

- They're cute! They're really small.
- Thanks! They were born in February.
- Were they born in a hospital?
- Yes, they were. Were you born in a hospital, too?
- No, I wasn't. I was born at home.
- And I was born in a jungle!

DISCOVER GRAMMAR

Circle.
I **was** / **were**
You **was** / **were** born.
They **was** / **were**

2 Look at Activity 1. Circle *Yes* or *No*.

1. Were the babies born in August?   Yes / No
2. Were they born in February?   Yes / No
3. Were they born in a hospital?   Yes / No

3 Talk to a friend.

1. When were you born?
2. Were you born in a hospital?
3. Were you born at home?

- When were you born?
- I was born in ...

WORKBOOK page 60

GRAMMAR GUIDE page 132

Lesson 3 — SOUNDS AND SPELLING

TRACK 70

1 Listen to the poem.

dr ld gr

My grandpa's really great
And he's very, very old.
He has an old green coat,
He wears it when it's cold.

He drives an old green car
When he comes to visit me.
He tells me lots of stories,
And drinks a cup of tea.

2 Circle, sort, and write.

grandpa drink drive cold green old

dr	ld	gr
_____	_____	_____
_____	_____	_____

3 Write a word with *dr*, *ld*, or *gr*.

❶ _____   ❷ _____   ❸ _____

WORKBOOK page 61

Lesson 4 · READING TIME·

TRACK 71

1 Listen and read.

1. It's very green here. There are lots of sheep.
Hey! Sheep don't like drinking soda. Don't drop litter!

2. There are lots of cows here.
There's an old bull, too! Close the gate! Run!

3. Ouch!
Don't pick wild flowers. They're important for bees.

4. Now, please remember, respect the environment.
We know, Grandpa. Don't drop litter, close the gates, and don't pick wild flowers.

2 Read the story again. Check (✓) the **value**.

Respect: Respect the environment. ◯   Don't drop litter. ◯

3 Do you respect the environment? Circle what you do.

I never drop litter. / I don't pick wild flowers. / I respect animals.

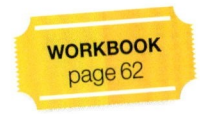

WORKBOOK page 62

95

Lesson 5

VOCABULARY

TRACK 72

1 Listen, point, and say.

1. happy
2. sad 
3. tired 
4. bored 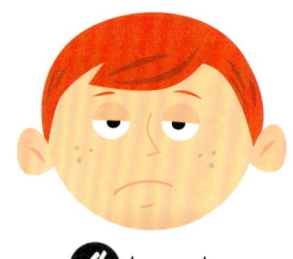
5. excited 
6. scared 
7. mad 

TRACK 73

2 Listen and act.

TRACK 74

3 Listen and complete. Then sing. **In Your Dreams**

Last night, in your dreams,
Were you big?
Were you small?
Were you _____?
Were you _____?

Last night, in your dreams,
Were you happy?
Were you _____?
Were you tired?
Were you _____?

Lesson 6

GRAMMAR

You / They **were** at an airport.
You / They **weren't** happy.

TRACK 75

1 Listen, read, and say.

Look at my grandparents! They were pilots! They were at an airport.

Look, Zac! You were very small. You weren't very happy!

1974   2010

DISCOVER GRAMMAR

Circle.

They were(n't) sad tells us about **now** / **yesterday**.

You are(n't) tired tells us about **now** / **yesterday**.

2 Look at Activity 1. Then circle the correct words.

1 In 1974, Zac's grandparents   were / weren't   at an airport.
2 In 1974, Zac's grandparents   were / weren't   teachers.
3 In 2010, Zac   was / wasn't   small.
4 In 2010, Zac   was / wasn't   young.

3 Look around your classroom. Act it out and say.

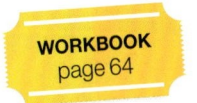

You were in front of the board.

WORKBOOK page 64

GRAMMAR GUIDE page 132

Lesson 7

FACTUAL READER

LET'S VISIT THE USA

1 Read about movie stars in the USA.

www.movie-stars.com

The USA is the home of the movies, and lots of movie stars live and work in Hollywood, California. Many actors are very talented – they can act happy or sad, friendly or mad, excited or bored.

The most important award for an actor is the famous Oscar. Every year, there is an awards ceremony in February or March. There's also a road in Hollywood called the Hollywood Walk of Fame, where many famous people have "stars" on the sidewalk. Some movie stars make prints of their hands and feet in front of a famous theater.

It's a fact!

The youngest person to win an acting Oscar was Tatum O'Neal. She was ten!

2 Read and write.

1 What emotions can actors act?
2 Where do famous actors make hand and footprints?

Think Twice

1 Who is your favorite movie star? Why do you like him / her?
2 Do you think awards are important for actors? Why? Why not?

Lesson 8

SPEAKING TIME

PRESENTATION: A FAMOUS ACTOR

1 Prepare.

Find information about the person.
Use the questions below to help you.

- Choose a famous actor to talk about.
- Draw or glue pictures of him / her, and add labels.
- Find information about him / her.

> Where is he / she from?
> Where does he / she work?
> Can you name a movie he / she is in?
> Who does he / she play?
> What emotions does he / she use in the movie?
> Do you like this actor?

2 Practice.

Describe your famous actor.

> Let me tell you about …

> His / Her name is …
> He / She is from …

> He / She works in …

> He / She is in the … and he / she acts …

> I like / don't like … because …

TRACK 76

3 Present.

> Let me tell you about my favorite movie star. His name is Ewan McGregor, and he's from Scotland. He works in Hollywood making movies. He's in the *Christopher Robin* and he acts the part of Christopher Robin himself! I like him because he's a great actor.

WORKBOOK page 65

UNIT 7 · PROGRESS CHECK ·

1 Look at the pictures and write. /5

1 soccer player **2** nurse **3** wrestler **4** pilot **5** firefighter **6** police officer

1 He's going to be a soccer player _____.
2 _____.
3 _____.
4 _____.
5 _____.
6 _____.

2 Look at the pictures and complete the story. /5

Today, I'm not going to school – it's Saturday! First **1** _I'm going to take a shower_ , and then **2** _____.

This morning, I'm going to **3** _____ and then I'm going to **4** _____.

This afternoon, I'm not going to **5** _____, it's finished! I'm going to **6** _____.

TOTAL /10

WORKBOOK page 66   STICKERS   PASSPORT page 14

PROGRESS CHECK

1 Complete the months. Then write answers for you. /6

1 Were you born in <u>M a y</u>? <u>No, I wasn't</u>.
2 Were you at school in O __ t __ b __ r? _____.
3 Was your teacher at school in J __ __ y? _____.
4 Were your friends in the mountains in F __ __ __ u __ __ y? _____.

2 Look at the picture and read. Then choose and write the correct word. /4

1 Yesterday was my birthday. I was very ____<u>happy</u>____ because it was my party.
2 But my friend Pete was _____ because there wasn't any cake.
3 My mom was _____ because the house was messy.
4 The party was great – lots of games and we weren't _____.
5 At the end, we were very _____ and sleepy.

1 **a** (happy)   **b** sad   **c** tired   4 **a** excited   **b** scared   **c** bored

2 **a** happy   **b** tired   **c** sad   5 **a** mad   **b** bored   **c** tired

3 **a** mad   **b** excited **c** happy

TOTAL /10

WORKBOOK page 67   STICKERS   PASSPORT page 16

FRANCE

STEAM

TEAM NAME

What is a catapult, and what is it for?

1 Get materials.

rubber bands   7 craft sticks   plastic spoon   pompom balls   markers

2 Add color to sticks.

3 Wrap rubber bands around sticks.

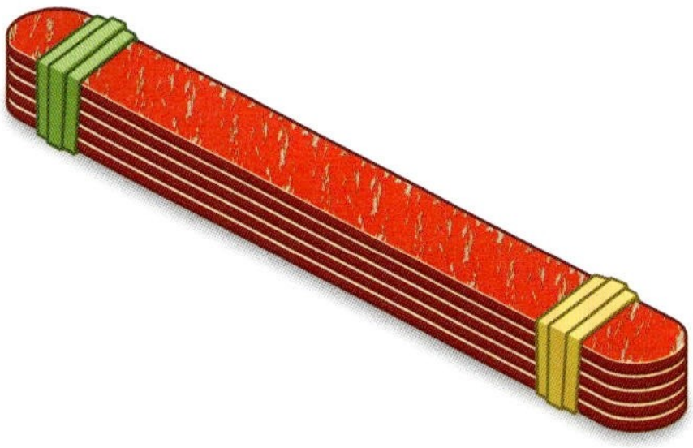

1 around each end of 5 sticks 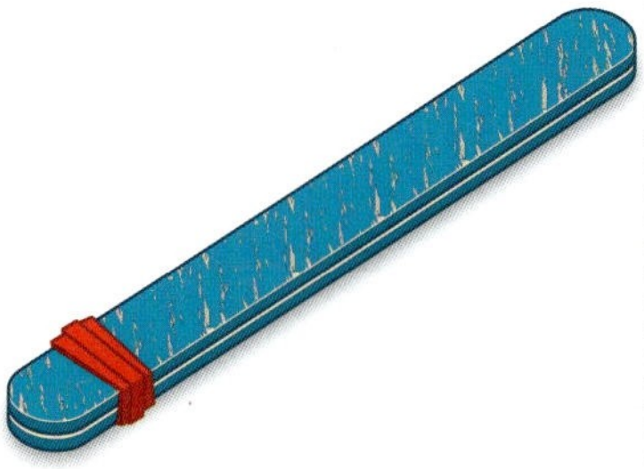   2 around one end of 2 sticks

Catapults are levers. Seesaws and scissors are also levers.

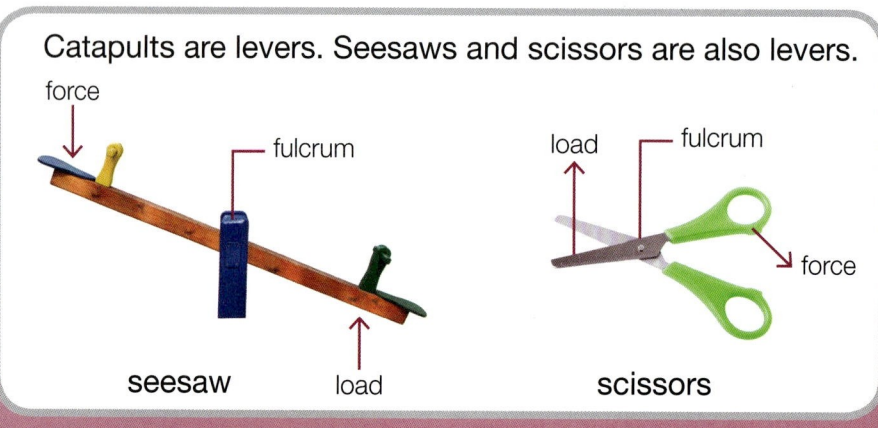

force — fulcrum
seesaw — load

load — fulcrum — force
scissors

Medieval balls used in catapults in the 13th century.

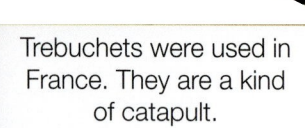

Trebuchets were used in France. They are a kind of catapult.

Replica of a catapult in Baux-de-Provence.

102

CHALLENGE 4

· BUILD A CATAPULT ·

USA

4 Assemble your catapult.

1 Pull the two sticks apart. Put the 5 sticks inside.

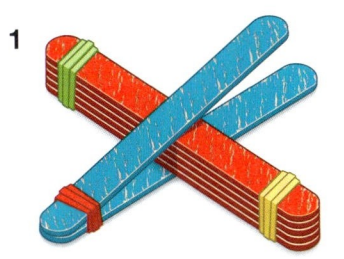

2 Make an X with a rubber band connecting the stack of 5 to the top stick.

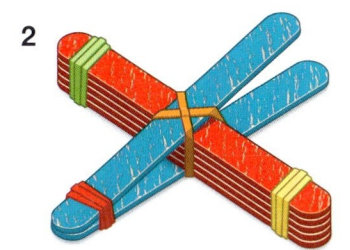

3 Attach a plastic spoon to the top stick with rubber bands.

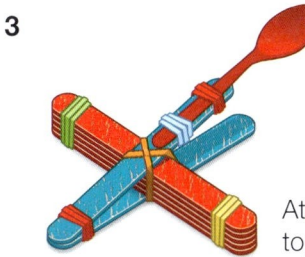

5 Place a pompom on the spoon.

6 Hold the catapult, press down, and release!

Name the fulcrum, the load, and the force in the catapult.

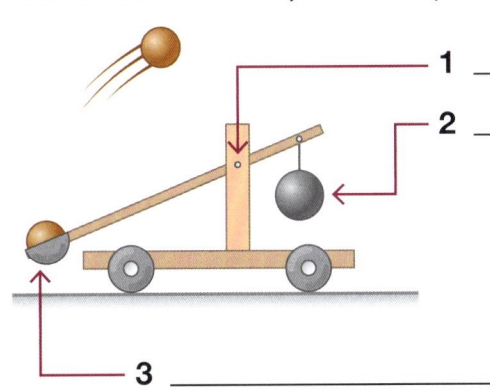

1 _____
2 _____
3 _____

Pumpkins are used in catapult competitions.

Pumpkins are launched on a trebuchet in California.

Students in a catapult competition at Snake River High School, Idaho.

Super Star Challenge
Create targets for your catapults like hoops or cups.

TEAMWORK ★★★★★

MOROCCO

UNIT 9

We're in Morocco! It's fascinating here!

Morocco is a very hot country near the Sahara Desert. There are lots of colorful markets in Morocco.

Which continent is Morocco in?
Can you find it on a map?
How many languages do they speak in Morocco?
Do you have any markets like this in your country?

Zoom in

Look at the picture.
What food can you buy?

UNIT 9

Lesson 1 · VOCABULARY ·

1 Listen, point, and say.

1. seven thirty
2. a quarter after ten 
3. a quarter to three 
4. midnight 
5. noon 

2 Listen and draw the times on the clocks. Then write.

1. I was at the club at _____.
2. I was at the library at _____. 
3. I was at the pool at _____. 
4. I was in bed at _____. 

3 Choose a time and talk to a friend.

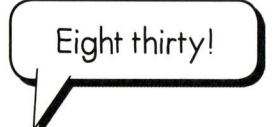

Eight thirty!

I was at school.

WORKBOOK page 68

Lesson 2

TRACK 79

1 Listen, read, and say.

GRAMMAR

I / He / She was in the city.
I / He / She wasn't at the flower market.

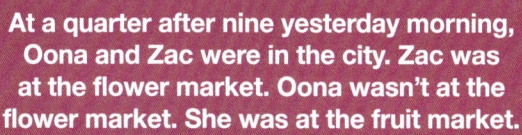

At a quarter after nine yesterday morning, Oona and Zac were in the city. Zac was at the flower market. Oona wasn't at the flower market. She was at the fruit market.

At a quarter to eleven, they were on the bus.

Look! I was at the flower market.

I wasn't at the flower market. I was at the fruit market …

DISCOVER GRAMMAR

Circle the correct alternatives.

Yesterday, **I / you / he / she / it / we / they** was in the park.

2 Circle *True* or *False*.

1 At a quarter to nine, Zac was at the flower market.   True / False
2 At a quarter after nine, Zac was at the flower market.   True / False
3 At a quarter after nine, Oona was at the fruit market.   True / False
4 At ten o'clock, they were on the bus.   True / False

3 Talk about yourself.

Yesterday afternoon, at two thirty, I was … / I wasn't …

Yesterday evening, at a quarter after eight, I was … / I wasn't …

WORKBOOK page 69

GRAMMAR GUIDE page 133

Lesson 3 — SOUNDS AND SPELLING

air ou oy

1 Listen and chant.

I have fair hair and a pair of blue eyes.

I can shout with my mouth — shout out loud!

This boy, Roy, is playing with his toys.

2 Listen and complete. Then cross (✗) out the word with a different sound.

1. h _a_ _i_ _r_
   b __ __
   t __ __
   _____

2. m __ __ t h
   t __ __
   s h __ __ t
   _____

3. p __ __ __
   h __ __ __
   m __ __ t h
   _____

3 Look back at the chant. Find one more word for each column.

Lesson 4

READING TIME

1 Listen and read.

1
- Where's the chocolate cake? It was here this morning!
- Um ...
- Look at your mouth! You're a greedy boy!

2
- Look at my hair gel! It's empty!
- Uhh ... Sorry, Dad. Don't shout!

3
- Where are my toys? They were here earlier.
- Um, sorry ...

4
- But I love your toys!

2 Read the story again. Check (✓) the **value**.

Responsibility: Follow the example of others. ◯   Set a good example. ◯

3 What do you do to set a good example? Read and check (✓).

I am on time for school. ◯   I do my homework. ◯

I clean my room. ◯   I am polite to everyone. ◯

WORKBOOK page 71

Lesson 5 · VOCABULARY ·

TRACK 83

1 Listen, point, and say.

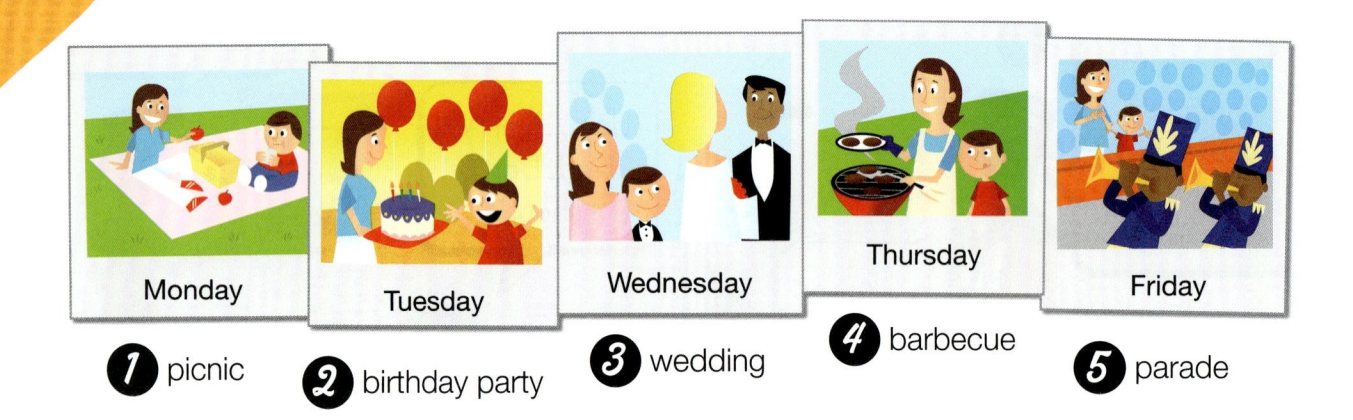

Monday — **1** picnic
Tuesday — **2** birthday party
Wednesday — **3** wedding
Thursday — **4** barbecue
Friday — **5** parade

2 Remember and circle *True* or *False*.

1 They were at a wedding on Wednesday. (True) / False
2 They were at a birthday party on Tuesday. True / False
3 They were at a barbecue on Friday. True / False
4 They were at a parade on Monday. True / False
5 They were at a picnic on Thursday. True / False

3 Draw a picture of an event you were at last year. Then play a guessing game.

— Were you at a barbecue?
— No, I wasn't.
— Were you at a wedding?
— Yes, I was.

WORKBOOK page 72

Lesson 6

1 Listen, read, and say.

GRAMMAR

Was **he / she / it** at a barbecue?
Yes, **he / she / it was.**
No, **he / she / it wasn't.**

Yesterday

Today

Was Oona at a birthday party yesterday?

No, she wasn't.

Was she at a barbecue?

Yes, she was.

DISCOVER GRAMMAR

Match the three columns.

In a statement with *be* we use   subject + verb   **Was he / she … ?**
In a question with *be* we use   verb + subject   **He / She was …**

2 Look at Activity 1. Ask and answer.

3 Listen and complete. Then sing. **The Mystery Song**

_____ he at a barbecue?

_____ she at the zoo?

Where *were* they?

_____ they with you?

He _____ at a barbecue,

She _____ at the zoo.

Where _____ they?

They _____ with you!

Lesson 7

·FACTUAL READER·

LET'S VISIT MOROCCO

1 Read about a wedding in Morocco.

Yesterday was a special day for 10-year-old Afdal Eddine. It was his sister's wedding day. Weddings are very special in Morocco.

It's a fact!

Some women in Morocco take a bath in milk before their wedding!

Before the ceremony, there was a team of chefs to prepare delicious meals for family members and friends. There were more than 100 guests at the wedding.

Afdal's sister was beautiful in her traditional dress and jewels. Her hands and feet were painted in henna with special designs for good luck.

There was music and singing and dancing all night, and there were many visitors from different villages. It was very exciting for Afdal!

2 Read and write.

1 What happened during the wedding?

2 Can you describe Afdal's sister on her wedding day?

Think Twice

1 Do you know any other ceremonies with singing and dancing?

2 Are weddings similar in your country?

Lesson 8

SPEAKING TIME

PRESENTATION: A SPECIAL CEREMONY IN YOUR COUNTRY

1 Prepare.

Find information about the ceremony. Use the questions below to help you.

- Choose a special ceremony to talk about.
- Draw or glue pictures of it, and add labels.
- Find information about it.

What happens before the ceremony?

What kind of food do people eat?

How many people attend the ceremony?

What do people wear?

What do people do?

2 Practice.

Describe your ceremony.

Let me tell you about …

Normally, … people attend the ceremony.

… wear(s) …

… present(s) …

… the ceremony, people …

3 Present.

TRACK 86

Let me tell you about our school graduation ceremony. Normally, about 200 people attend the ceremony. The boys wear suits, and the girls wear dresses. The parents watch, and the teachers present pieces of paper called degrees. After the ceremony, people have big parties.

WORKBOOK page 74

VIETNAM

WELCOME TO VIETNAM

I'm in Vietnam. Look at her hat!

Unit 10

The girl is from Vietnam. She's wearing a traditional hat to protect her from the sun and the rain.

Which countries are next to Vietnam on a map?
What is the weather like in Vietnam?
Do you have traditional clothes in your country? What are they?

ZOOM IN

Look at the picture.
Where do you think the girl is?

Lesson 1

VOCABULARY

TRACK 87

1 Listen, point, and say.

1 furniture
2 toys
3 animals
4 food
5 money
6 clothes

TRACK 88

2 Listen and say *It's …* or *They're …*

3 Label the groups and complete with words from the box.

| ~~dollars~~ | chair | ball | T-shirt | cat | sandwich |
| cents | table | dog | pants | robot | apple |

money

_____dollars_____
_____
_____

_____
_____
_____

_____
_____
_____

_____
_____
_____

_____
_____
_____

_____
_____
_____

WORKBOOK page 75

Lesson 2

TRACK 89

1 Listen, read, and say.

GRAMMAR

There was some furniture.
There was a horse.
There were some flowers.

This morning, Zac was at a parade.

Where were you this morning, Zac?

I was at the parade. It was fun! There were some animals and there was a horse! There was some food, too.

DISCOVER GRAMMAR

Circle.

We use **there was** / **there were** to talk about one thing.
We use **there was** / **there were** to talk about two or more things.
We use **there was** / **there were** to talk about things we can't count.

2 Complete the sentences.

1 _____There were_____ some flags.
2 _____ a horse.
3 _____ some food.
4 _____ some flowers.

There were three pencils. There was some money. And there was one ruler.

3 Play a memory game.

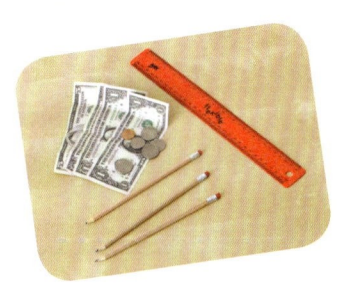

WORKBOOK page 76

GRAMMAR GUIDE page 133

UNIT 10

Lesson 3

SOUNDS AND SPELLING

TRACK 90

1 Listen to the poem.

| sm | sc | tr |

I'm a sailor on the seas,
And I'm traveling for pleasure.
I can see a small island,
Maybe there's some treasure!

Now I'm on the island,
It's scary and it's still.
I see trees, birds, and fruit,
But I'm hungry and ill.

There's some smoke in the trees.
I think I see a house,
Wait! I hear an animal.
A scorpion? No, a mouse!

2 Circle, sort, and write.

scaredtreesmallscorpionsmoketravel

sm	sc	tr
_____	_____	_____
_____	_____	_____

3 Write a word with *sm*, *sc*, or *tr*.

❶ _____ ❷ _____ ❸ _____

118

WORKBOOK page 77

Lesson 4 ·READING TIME·

1 Listen and read.

1 Look! A small island. We can try here!

2 In July, the sailors were happy. There was food for everyone. There were fish in the ocean, and there was fruit on the trees.

3 But in January, there wasn't any food. The sailors were hungry and scared.
— What are we going to eat?
— I don't know.

4 Some natives were nearby.
— We have some food.
— Let's help them.

5 They were generous and they were friendly. And there was food for everyone again.
— You are true friends.

6 Now the sailors weren't hungry or scared. They were happy.
— Smile, please.

2 Read the story again. Check (✓) the **value**.

Solidarity: Help those in need. ◯   Help your friends. ◯

3 Do you help those in need? Read and write *Yes* or *No*.

I help my family. _____   I visit friends if they are sick. _____

I share my food with hungry people. _____

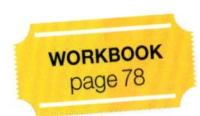

WORKBOOK page 78

UNIT 10

Lesson 5

VOCABULARY

TRACK 92

1 Listen, point, and say.

1. spring
2. summer
3. fall
4. winter
5. snow
6. ice
7. water

2 Circle and say.

1. Ice is   hot. / cold.
2. Snow is   hot. / cold.
3. People can ski in   the winter. / the summer.
4. Fish can swim in   snow. / water.

3 Write about the weather in your city. Then talk to a friend.

1. Is it cold in winter? _____.
2. Is it rainy in summer? _____.
3. In winter, is there any ice on the rivers? _____.
4. In spring, is there any snow? _____.
5. In fall, are there leaves on the sidewalk? _____.

WORKBOOK page 79

Is it cold in winter?

Lesson 6

TRACK 93

1 Listen, read, and say.

GRAMMAR

How much food **was there**?
How many children **were there**?

- I was at a great party last night.
- How much food was there?
- There was lots of food.
- How many children were there?
- There weren't any children, but there were lots of animals!

DISCOVER GRAMMAR

Circle.
We use **how much** / **how many** to ask about things we can count.
We use **how much** / **how many** to ask about things we can't count.

TRACK 94

2 Listen and complete. Then sing. **Last Summer**

Last summer …

How _____ water _____ _____ in the pool?
There was lots. There was lots and lots.

How _____ children _____ _____ at school?
There weren't any. There weren't any at all.

Last spring …

How _____ leaves _____ _____ on the trees?
There were lots. There were lots and lots.

How _____ ice _____ _____ in the pool?
There wasn't any. There wasn't any at all.

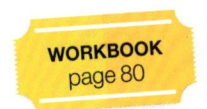

WORKBOOK page 80   **GRAMMAR GUIDE** page 133

121

Unit 10 · Lesson 7 · FACTUAL READER

LET'S VISIT VIETNAM

1 Read about water puppets in Vietnam.

www.water-puppets.com

Hello, friends!

This week, I want to tell you about a very original kind of theater in my country. Vietnam is a very rainy place – it rains in winter, spring, summer, and fall. Water is very important in Vietnam. There are lots of rivers and rice paddy fields, and there is a lot of water everywhere. More than a thousand years ago, rice farmers were in the fields all day. For entertainment, they invented water puppets. Water puppet shows are stories about everyday life in Vietnamese villages. They are very funny! Today, there are water puppet shows in special theaters. My favorite characters are the animals and dragons. The audience can get very wet at a water puppet show!

It's a fact!

Sometimes the dragon puppets can look like they are breathing fire!

2 Read and write.

1 When does it rain in Vietnam?

2 What do you find out about water puppet shows?

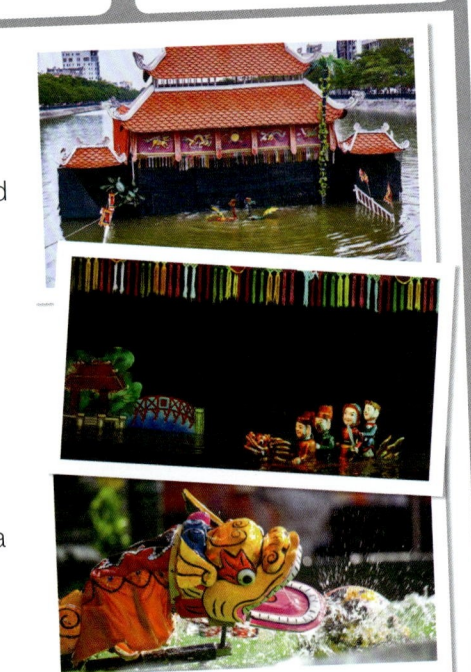

Think Twice

1 Do you think water puppet shows are fun? Why?

2 Are there any traditional puppet shows in your country? Describe them.

Lesson 8 ·SPEAKING TIME·

PRESENTATION: A TRADITIONAL SHOW FROM YOUR COUNTRY

1 Prepare.

Find information about the show.
Use the questions below to help you.

- Choose a special type of show to talk about.
- Draw or glue pictures of it, and add labels.
- Find information about it.

What part of your country is it from?

How old is it?   What kind of characters are there?

Where is it performed?   Do you like this kind of show / performance? Why / Why not?

2 Practice.

Describe your show.

Let me tell you about …

It's performed in …

It's from …

Characters are …

I like / don't like … because …

TRACK 95

3 Present.

Let me tell you about a traditional puppet show in Turkey. It's performed in the villages, but originally it was from a city called Bursa. Typical characters are men and animals. I like it because it's fun.

WORKBOOK page 81

PROGRESS CHECK

1 Look at the pictures and read the story. Then answer the questions. /5

Monday Wednesday Friday

Saturday Sunday

Andy was very busy this week. On Monday, he was at a picnic with his friend Jamie. On Wednesday, he was at the holiday parade. On Friday, Andy was at his birthday party with all his friends. On Saturday, Andy and his sister were at their cousin's wedding. On Sunday, Andy was at a family barbecue. Yummy!

1 Was Andy at a wedding on Monday? No, he wasn't. He was at a picnic.
2 Was he at a birthday party on Wednesday? _____.
3 Where was Andy on Friday? _____.
4 Where was Andy on Saturday? _____.
5 Was Jamie at the barbecue with Andy? _____.

What is the best name for this story? Check (✓) one box.

Andy's birthday party ◯ Andy's vacation ◯ Andy's busy week ◯

2 Now write answers for you. /5

1 Were you at school at 9 o'clock today? _____.
2 Were you at home yesterday at 4 o'clock? _____.
3 Were you at a party on Saturday? _____.
4 Was your best friend at your birthday party? _____.
5 Was your teacher at school on Sunday? _____.

TOTAL /10

UNIT 10

PROGRESS CHECK

1 Unscramble the words. Then write sentences. /4

1 syto _____ There were some toys _____.
2 tunrfeuir _____ There was some furniture _____.
3 nemoy _____.
4 minalas _____.
5 selothc _____.
6 ofod _____.

2 Sort the words into two lists. /6

water   eggs   bread   bananas   nurses   sausages   snow
parties   soup   chocolate   cupcakes   ice   grapes   milk

How much | How many
water | bananas
_____ | _____
_____ | _____
_____ | _____
_____ | _____
_____ | _____

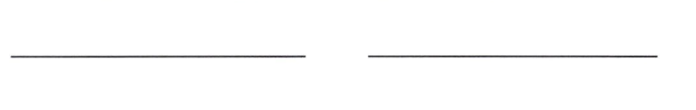

TOTAL /10

WORKBOOK page 83   STICKERS   PASSPORT page 20

MOROCCO

STEAM

TEAM NAME

What type of materials do we use in art?

1 Get materials.

- styrofoam tray
- plastic tray
- paper
- pencil
- gouache paint
- paint roller
- scissors
- glue stick
- colored paper

Super Star Challenge

2 Design your picture on a piece of paper before drawing it on the styrofoam.

Zellige tiles cut by hand in Fez, Morocco.

Artists use skill and design to create each Zellige.

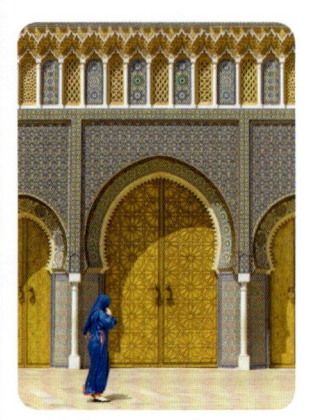

Zellige mosaics are used to decorate the facades of palaces.

Zellige tiles appeared in Morocco in the 10th century and are still used on buildings. The Hassan II Mosque is an example.

Dong Ho painting originated in Dong Ho Village. Each print tells a story. These folk paintings are usually displayed in homes and stores at the Lunar New Year.

CHALLENGE 5

PRINT A PICTURE

VIETNAM

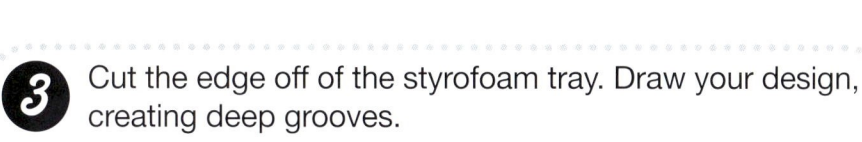

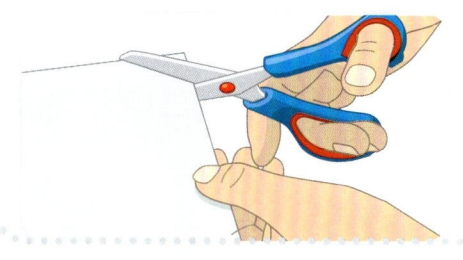

3 Cut the edge off of the styrofoam tray. Draw your design, creating deep grooves.

4 Put paint on the plastic tray. Then spread it over the styrofoam using the paint roller.

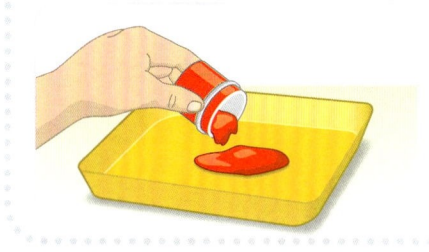

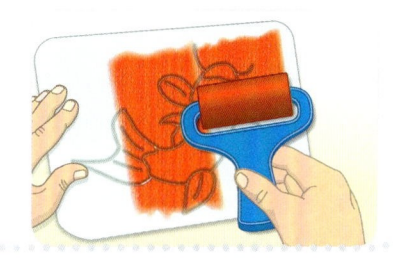

5 Press the paper firmly. Lift it and let it dry.

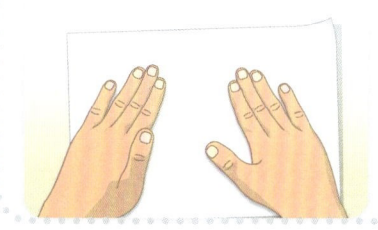

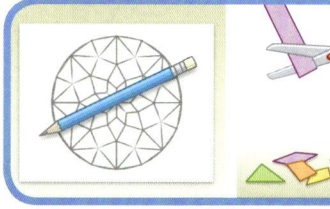

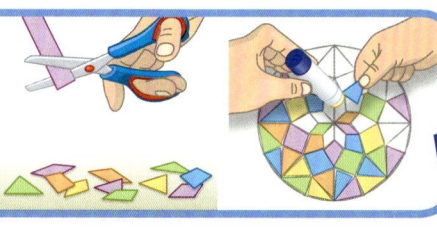

Can you find examples of these art techniques in your culture: sculpture, carving, mosaics, or printing?

Super Star Challenge
Make a paper mosaic.

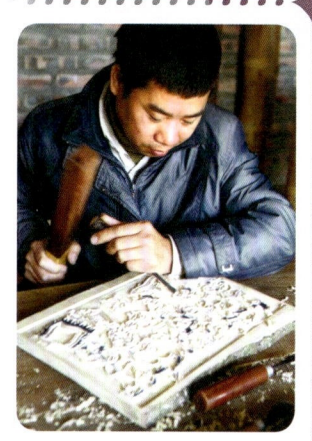

Dong Ho artist carving a woodblock in Dong Ho Village, Vietnam.

An artist printing pictures onto homemade paper.

Dong Ho woodblock print of a female warrior.

TEAMWORK

· GRAMMAR GUIDE ·

HOW TO USE THE GRAMMAR GUIDE

Hello! I'm Gabi! I'm your Grammar Guide for this level. I love grammar! Grammar is great and grammar is easy! I'm here to help you with all the grammar in your book. Come and visit me after each grammar lesson!

GABI'S HOME STUDY GUIDE

1. Read your Grammar Guide again at home.
2. Look at the example. Close your book. Try to say the example.
3. Open your book and check.
4. Make new examples to practice.

1 After your grammar lesson, turn to the Grammar Guide. Look at the example.

Let's go to the zoo!
Let's go by train.

2 Complete the activity. Use the example to help you.

Complete the sentences.

1 _____ bike.

2 _____ the park.

3 _____ the desert.

4 _____ plane.

5 _____ car.

3 Check your answers.

Come back and see me if you get lost!

128

UNIT 1 MEXICO

Lesson 2

Let's go to the zoo!
Let's go by train.

Complete the sentences.

1 _____ bike.
2 _____ the park.
3 _____ the desert.
4 _____ plane.
5 _____ car.

Lesson 6

The park is **next to** the castle.
The city is **in front of** the pyramid.
The pyramid is **behind** the city.

Complete the sentences with one word.

1 The city is _____ to the ocean.
2 The jungle is _____ the city.
3 The city is in _____ of the jungle.
4 The ocean is next _____ the city.
5 The jungle isn't _____ front of the city.

UNIT 2 SOUTH AFRICA

Lesson 2

There are some eggs.
There aren't any grapes.

Complete the sentences.

1 There aren't _____ pears.
2 _____ are some sausages.
3 _____ are _____ cherries.
4 There _____ any cookies.
5 _____ aren't _____ cupcakes.

Lesson 6

There's some bread.
There isn't any soup.

Is there any cheese?
Yes, **there is**. / No, **there isn't**.

Match.

1 There's   a any bread.
2 There isn't   b any soup?
3 Is there   c there isn't.
4 There's some   d chocolate.
5 Yes,   e some soda.
6 No,   f there is.

UNIT 3 MALAYSIA

Lesson 2

Where are you from?
I'm from Spain. / **I'm** Spanish.

Where's he / she from?
He's / She's from Spain.
He's / She's Spanish.

Complete the sentences.

1 _____ he _____? _____ from Turkey.

2 He's _____ Japan. _____ Japanese.

3 Where's _____ _____? She's _____ South Korea.

4 Where _____ you _____? I'm from _____.

Lesson 6

Dance with me / us / them / him / her.
Let's dance with him / her / them.
Can I help you?
Climb it / them.

Circle.

1 Open <u>the window</u>, please. it / me

2 Can you help <u>my sister and me</u>, please? you / us

3 Peter is with <u>Gabi</u>. him / her

4 Can I write to <u>Peter and Gabi</u>? them / you

5 I like <u>strawberries</u>. them / us

UNIT 4 ITALY

Lesson 2

I'm sailing.   **We're play**ing.
I'm not fishing.   **We aren't swimm**ing.

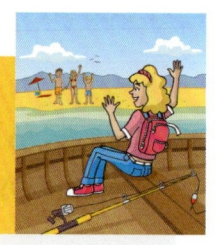

Complete the sentences.

1 (We / not / fish) _____ at the beach.
   (We / surf) _____ in the ocean.

2 (I / not / skate) _____ at the park.
   (I / ski) _____ in the mountains.

3 (I / not / climb) _____ in the mountains.
   (I / walk) _____ in the jungle.

Lesson 6

Are you playing baseball?
Yes, **I am.** / No, **I'm not.**
Are they playing baseball?
Yes, **they are.** / No, **they aren't.**

Complete the sentences.

1 _____ they running? Yes, they _____.

2 Are _____ eating? No, I'm _____.

3 _____ they talking? No, they _____.

4 _____ you writing? Yes, _____ _____.

UNIT 5 JAMAICA

Lesson 2

What's he / she / it doing?
He's / She's / It's eat**ing** a banana.
He / She / It isn't eat**ing** a sandwich.

Complete the sentences.

1 _____ the monkey _____? _____ eating.

2 What's Gabi _____? _____ sleeping.

3 _____ the bird _____? _____ singing.

4 Zac _____ reading a book. _____ writing.

Lesson 6

Is he / she wear**ing** a hat?
Yes **he / she is**. / No **he / she isn't**.

Complete the questions and answers.

1 (he / wear) _____ a skirt? No, _____ _____.

2 (she / eat) _____ a banana? Yes, _____ _____.

3 (Paul / read) _____ a book? _____, _____ isn't.

4 (Gabi / ride) _____ a bike? _____, _____ is.

UNIT 6 CHILE

Lesson 2

Where are you going?
Are you going to the library?
No, **I'm not. I'm going to** the movie theater.
Are you going to the movie theater? Yes, **I am**!
They are going to the movie theater.

Match.

1 Where   a   you going to the pool?
2 Are   b   I'm not.
3 No,   c   I am.
4 They   d   are they going?
5 Yes,   e   are going to the museum.

Lesson 6

Where is he going?
He's going to the stadium.

Is she going to the stadium, too?
No, **she isn't**.

Complete the sentences.

1 _____ is she going?

2 _____ he going _____ the pool? No, _____ _____.

3 Is _____ _____ to _____ stadium? _____, he is.

4 Where is _____ _____?

UNIT 7 FRANCE

Lesson 2

Are you going to be a police officer?
No, **I'm not. I'm going to be a** vet.
Are you going to be a vet?
Yes, **I am!**

Complete the sentences.

1 _____ you going to _____ a nurse? _____, I am.

2 Are you _____ _____ be a teacher? _____, _____ not.

3 I'm going _____ _____ _____ writer.

Lesson 6

On Saturday **he / she's going to** take a shower.
He / She isn't going to play soccer.
Is he / she going to watch TV on Saturday?
Yes, **he / she is.**
Is he / she going to use the Internet?
No, **he / she isn't.**

Match.

1 He's   a isn't going to watch TV.
2 She   b he is.
3 Is   c going to play soccer.
4 Yes,   d he going to read a book?
5 No,   e she isn't.

UNIT 8 USA

Lesson 2

I was born in a hospital.
Were you born in March?
No, **I wasn't.** / Yes, **I was!**
Were they born in March?
Yes, **they were.** / No, **they weren't.**

Complete the sentences.

1 _____ you born _____ August? No, I _____.

2 I _____ born _____ April. I was _____ in March.

3 Were _____ born _____ a hospital? Yes, they _____.

Lesson 6

You were at the beach yesterday. **You weren't** at school.
They were at the airport. **They weren't** at home.

Unscramble and write the sentences.

1 at yesterday home weren't You
_____.

2 were the You stadium at
_____.

3 grandparents weren't Gabi's teachers
_____.

Unit 9 MOROCCO

Lesson 2

I / He / She was at the flower market yesterday.
I / He / She wasn't at the mall.

Write *was* or *wasn't*.

1 Gabi _____ at the flower market yesterday.
2 She _____ with her friends.
3 She _____ with her parents.

Lesson 6

Was he / she at the party?
Yes, **he / she was.** / No, **he / she wasn't.**
Was the dog at the party?
Yes, **it was.** / No, **it wasn't.**

Complete the sentences.

1 _____ it rainy yesterday?
No, _____ _____.

2 _____ your sister at the party?
Yes, _____ _____.

3 _____ the party fun?
Yes, _____ _____.

4 Where _____ John yesterday?
_____ was at the zoo.

Unit 10 VIETNAM

Lesson 2

There was some food.
There was a horse.
There were some elephants.

Circle the correct words.

1 There **was / were a / some** animals.
2 There **was / were a / some** food.
3 There **was / were a / some** flag.
4 There **was / were one / some** horse.
5 There **was / were a / three** elephants.

Lesson 6

How much water **was there**?
There was lots. / There wasn't any.
How many trees **were there**?
There were lots. / There weren't any.

Complete the sentences.

1 How _____ flowers _____ there? _____ _____ lots.

2 _____ _____ children were _____? There _____ any.

3 _____ _____ leaves _____ _____? _____ were lots.

4 _____ _____ ice _____ _____? _____ _____ any.

133

2020 © Macmillan Education do Brasil

Based on *Next Move*
© Macmillan Publishers Limited 2013
Text © Cantabgilly Limited and Mary Charrington 2013
Adapted by Sue Clarke
Grammar Guide written by Sue Clarke
STEAM Challenge sections written by Sarah Elizabeth Sprague
Next Move is a registered trademark, property of Macmillan Publishers, 2013
First edition entitled "Next Stop" published 2009 by Macmillan Publishers

Director of Languages Brazil: Patrícia Souza De Luccia
Publishing Manager and Field Researcher: Patricia Muradas
Content Creation Coordinator: Cristina do Vale
Art Editor: Jean Aranha
Lead Editors: Ana Beatriz da Costa Moreira, Daniela Gonçala da Costa, Luciana Pereira da Silva
Content Editors: Millyane M. Moura Moreira, Tarsílio Soares Moreira
Digital Editor: Ana Paula Girardi
Editorial Assistant: Roberta Somera
Editorial Intern: Bruna Marques
Art Assistant: Denis Araujo
Art Intern: Jacqueline Alves
Graphic Production: Tatiane Romano, Thais Mendes P. Galvão
Proofreaders: Edward Willson, Márcia Leme, Sabrina Cairo Bileski
Design Concept: Design Divertido Artes Gráficas
Page Make-Up: Figurattiva Editorial
Photo Research: Marcia Sato
Image Processing: Jean Aranha, Jacqueline Alves, Denis Araujo
Audio: Argila Music, Núcleo de Criação
Cover Concept: Jean Aranha
Cover photography: extravagantni/iStockphoto/Getty Images, Bubert/iStockphoto/Getty Images, LokFung/iStockphoto/Getty Images.
Commissioned photography: Macmillan Publishers Ltd/Paul Bricknell (15, 17, 41, 45, 49, 65, 75, 82, 89, 97, 99, 110, 113, 117, 123).
Map: Allmaps
Illustrations: Adilson Secco (p. 30-31, 55, 79, 102-103, 127), Gabriele Antonini | Advocate Art (p. 13, 23, 37, 47, 61, 71, 85, 95, 119), Fiona Gowen (p. 22, 28, 29, 37, 46, 53, 58, 61, 94, 100), Anna Hancock | Beehive (p. 12, 22, 36, 46, 60, 70, 84, 94, 108, 118), David Hurtado (p. 12, 22, 25, 36, 46, 52, 53, 60, 70, 76, 77, 84, 86, 94, 101, 108, 118, 128, 129, 130, 131, 132, 133), Gerald Kelley (p. 4, 8, 10, 11, 15, 16, 17, 18, 21, 25, 26, 27, 32, 35, 39, 40, 41, 45, 49, 50, 51, 59, 63, 64, 65, 69, 73, 74, 75, 83, 87, 88, 89, 92, 93, 97, 98, 99, 107, 111, 112, 113, 117, 121, 122, 123), Rob McClurkan (14, 20, 34, 38, 44, 48, 58, 62, 68, 72, 82, 86, 92, 96, 106, 110, 116, 120), Mark Ruffle | The Organisation (p. 11, 24, 25, 28, 29, 35, 45, 52, 53, 63, 69, 73, 76, 77, 100, 101, 111, 121, 124, 125).

Reproduction prohibited. Penal Code Article 184 and Law number 9.610 of February 19, 1998.

We would like to dedicate this book to teachers all over Brazil. We would also like to thank our clients and teachers who have helped us make this book better with their many rich contributions and feedback straight from the classroom!

The authors and publishers would like to thank the following for permission to reproduce the photographic material:
p. 8: Tunatura/iStockphoto/Getty Images; p. 11: gpointstudio/iStockphoto/Getty Images, andresr/iStockphoto/Getty Images, Spotmatik/iStockphoto/Getty Images, Cameris/iStockphoto/Getty Images; p. 14: blanscape/iStockphoto/Getty Images, gbh007/iStockphoto/Getty Images, alvarez/iStockphoto/Getty Images, PeopleImages/iStockphoto/Getty Images, Mixmike/iStockphoto/Getty Images, SolStock/iStockphoto/Getty Images; p. 16: venemama/iStockphoto/Getty Images, wrangel/iStockphoto/Getty Images; p. 17: purple_queue/iStockphoto/Getty Images, anankkml/iStockphoto/Getty Images, Michael Roeder/iStockphoto/Getty Images; p. 19: Amy Sparwasser/iStockphoto/Getty Images; p. 22: hayatikayhan/iStockphoto/Getty Images, PetrBonek/iStockphoto/Getty Images, goir/iStockphoto/Getty Images; p. 26: mantaphoto/iStockphoto/Getty Images, filrom/iStockphoto/Getty Images; p. 27: vitalssss/iStockphoto/Getty Images, slpu9945/iStockphoto/Getty Images, Laticka/iStockphoto/Getty Images; p. 30: Viktorcvetkovic/iStockphoto/Getty Images, stockcam/iStockphoto/Getty Images, Neal Simpson/EMPICS/Getty Images, AP Images/Glow Images, AP Images/Glow Images, DepositPhotos/Glow Images, Tolga TEZCAN/iStockphoto/Getty Images, natrot/iStockphoto/Getty Images, Lena Gadanski/iStockphoto/Getty Images, Santje09/iStockphoto/Getty Images; p. 31: flowgraph/iStockphoto/Getty Images, Frédéric Soltan/Corbis/Getty Images, AP Images/Glow Images, imageBROKER/Glow Images; p. 32: goc/iStockphoto/Getty Images; p. 35: Robbie Ross/iStockphoto/Getty Images, JBryson/iStockphoto/Getty Images; p. 36: julos/iStockphoto/Getty Images, WildLivingArts/iStockphoto/Getty Images, GOSPHOTODESIGN/iStockphoto/Getty Images; p. 38: cometary/iStockphoto/Getty Images, LightFieldStudios/iStockphoto/Getty Images, Dean Mitchell/iStockphoto/Getty Images, SolStock/iStockphoto/Getty Images, FG Trade/iStockphoto/Getty Images, imtmphoto/iStockphoto/Getty Images; p. 39: AwaylGl/iStockphoto/Getty Images, Balefire9/iStockphoto/Getty Images, eyewave/iStockphoto/Getty Images; p. 40: Marcos Calvo/iStockphoto/Getty Images, 7000/iStockphoto/Getty Images; p. 41: jenifoto/iStockphoto/Getty Images; p. 43: Dreamer Company/iStockphoto/Getty Images; p. 44: MaFelipe/iStockphoto/Getty Images, vitapix/iStockphoto/Getty Images, DieterMeyrl/iStockphoto/Getty Images, intst/iStockphoto/Getty Images, djjohn/iStockphoto/Getty Images, Fertnig/iStockphoto/Getty Images, SerrNovik/iStockphoto/Getty Images, supersizer/iStockphoto/Getty Images; p. 48: pepifoto/iStockphoto/Getty Images, skodonnell/iStockphoto/Getty Images, CrackerClips/iStockphoto/Getty Images, harmpeti/iStockphoto/Getty Images, MileA/iStockphoto/Getty Images, Alter_photo/iStockphoto/Getty Images, mixetto/iStockphoto/Getty Images, gyro/iStockphoto/Getty Images, Pixfly/iStockphoto/Getty Images; p. 50: Capuski/iStockphoto/Getty Images, kali9/iStockphoto/Getty Images; p. 51: South_agency/iStockphoto/Getty Images, JulieRob/iStockphoto/Getty Images, Hilch/iStockphoto/Getty Images; p. 54: Poligrafistka/iStockphoto/Getty Images, ErmakovaElena/iStockphoto/Getty Images, Dutko/iStockphoto/Getty Images, Richmatts/iStockphoto/Getty Images, Joel Carillet/iStockphoto/Getty Images, eZeePics Studio/iStockphoto/Getty Images, Devonyu/iStockphoto/Getty Images, george733/iStockphoto/Getty Images; Vadim Dorofeev/iStockphoto/Getty Images,

Eduard Lysenko/iStockphoto/Getty Images; p. 55: bodrumsurf/iStockphoto/Getty Images, maikid/iStockphoto/Getty Images, sbostock/iStockphoto/Getty Images, alxpin/iStockphoto/Getty Images; p. 56: isabeltp/iStockphoto/Getty Images; p. 58: bgfoto/iStockphoto/Getty Images, xxmmxx/iStockphoto/Getty Images, PaytonVanGorp/iStockphoto/Getty Images, ArtBoyMB/iStockphoto/Getty Images, Sadeugra/iStockphoto/Getty Images, Daniel Samray/iStockphoto/Getty Images, Marina79/iStockphoto/Getty Images; p. 62: Lalouetto/iStockphoto/Getty Images, Piotr Polaczyk/iStockphoto/Getty Images, studiocasper/iStockphoto/Getty Images, adisa/iStockphoto/Getty Images, Anna Egorova/iStockphoto/Getty Images, koya79/iStockphoto/Getty Images; p. 64: narvikk/iStockphoto/Getty Images, Wavebreakmedia/iStockphoto/Getty Images, peeterv/iStockphoto/Getty Images; p. 65: TriggerPhoto/iStockphoto/Getty Images, guenterguni/iStockphoto/Getty Images; p. 66: Easypix; p. 68: Steve Debenport/iStockphoto/Getty Images, Comeback Images/iStockphoto/Getty Images, FG Trade/iStockphoto/Getty Images, Trish233/iStockphoto/Getty Images, Deposit Photos/Glow Images, Image Source/iStockphoto/Getty Images, vchal/iStockphoto/Getty Images, CasarsaGuru/iStockphoto/Getty Images; p. 69: icefront/iStockphoto/Getty Images, londoneye/iStockphoto/Getty Images; p. 74: Gerold Grotelueschen/iStockphoto/Getty Images, JanRoode/iStockphoto/Getty Images, the-lightwriter/iStockphoto/Getty Images; p. 75: Maerie/iStockphoto/Getty Images, Meinzahn/iStockphoto/Getty Images; p. 78: Poligrafistka/iStockphoto/Getty Images, PytyCzech/iStockphoto/Getty Images, AP Images/Glow Images, master1305/iStockphoto/Getty Images, peeterv/iStockphoto/Getty Images, Rainer Lesniewski/iStockphoto/Getty Images, FrankRamspott/iStockphoto/Getty Images, Floortje/iStockphoto/Getty Images, Floortje/iStockphoto/Getty Images, kedsanee/iStockphoto/Getty Images, jldeines/iStockphoto/Getty Images, Michael Burrell/iStockphoto/Getty Images, Roman_Gorielov/iStockphoto/Getty Images, julichka/iStockphoto/Getty Images, Tolga TEZCAN/iStockphoto/Getty Images; p. 79: alexsl/iStockphoto/Getty Images, pop_jop/iStockphoto/Getty Images, stbaus7/iStockphoto/Getty Images, Grafissimo/iStockphoto/Getty Images, wastesoul/iStockphoto/Getty Images, subjug/iStockphoto/Getty Images, Floortje/iStockphoto/Getty Images; p. 80: AndreaAstes/iStockphoto/Getty Images; p. 86: ASIFE/iStockphoto/Getty Images, Louis-Paul St-Onge/iStockphoto/Getty Images, pamspix/iStockphoto/Getty Images, LSOphoto/iStockphoto/Getty Images, andresr/iStockphoto/Getty Images, JackF/iStockphoto/Getty Images, SergiyN/iStockphoto/Getty Images; p. 88: peplow/iStockphoto/Getty Images, monkeybusinessimages/iStockphoto/Getty Images, sergeyryzhov/iStockphoto/Getty Images, marieclaudelemay/iStockphoto/Getty Images; p. 89: Steve Debenport/iStockphoto/Getty Images, Steve Debenport/iStockphoto/Getty Images, Mr_Vector/iStockphoto/Getty Images; p. 90: Steve Debenport/iStockphoto/Getty Images; p. 92: MollyAnne/iStockphoto/Getty Images, gmnicholas/iStockphoto/Getty Images, spanteldotru/iStockphoto/Getty Images; p. 94: ithinksky/iStockphoto/Getty Images, janrysavy/iStockphoto/Getty Images, PicturePartners/iStockphoto/Getty Images; p. 96: skynesher/iStockphoto/Getty Images, Mario Anzuoni/Reuters/Latinstock, Ap Images/Glow Images; p. 97: Ap Images/Glow Images, Ap Images/Glow Images; p. 102: Inimma-IS/iStockphoto/Getty Images, CelesteQuest/iStockphoto/Getty Images, Lagui/iStockphoto/Getty Images, ivansmuk/iStockphoto/Getty Images, Bogdan Lytvynenko/iStockphoto/Getty Images, aee_werawan/iStockphoto/Getty Images, photka/iStockphoto/Getty Images, Tevarak/iStockphoto/Getty Images, p1images/iStockphoto/Getty Images, iJacky/iStockphoto/Getty Images; p. 103: alexsl/iStockphoto/Getty Images, MaRabelo/iStockphoto/Getty Images, MichiTermo/iStockphoto/Getty Images, Ap Images/Glow Images; p. 104: GoodLifeStudio/iStockphoto/Getty Images; p. 106: onlyyouqj/iStockphoto/Getty Images, YakobchukOlena/iStockphoto/Getty Images, andresr/iStockphoto/Getty Images, FangXiaNuo/iStockphoto/Getty Images, SeventyFour/iStockphoto/Getty Images, Wavebreak/iStockphoto/Getty Images; p. 108: ozgurdonmaz/iStockphoto/Getty Images, Zzvet/iStockphoto/Getty Images, SoumenNath/iStockphoto/Getty Images; p. 113: kali9/iStockphoto/Getty Images, fleaz/iStockphoto/Getty Images; p. 114: hadynyah/iStockphoto/Getty Images; p. 118: DragonImages/iStockphoto/Getty Images, scanrail/iStockphoto/Getty Images, CynthiaAnnF/iStockphoto/Getty Images; p. 120: tatyana_tomsickova/iStockphoto/Getty Images, kali9/iStockphoto/Getty Images, RiverNorthPhotography/iStockphoto/Getty Images, praetorianphoto/iStockphoto/Getty Images, BasSlabbers/iStockphoto/Getty Images, IRINA KROLEVETC/iStockphoto/Getty Images, DDurrich/iStockphoto/Getty Images; p. 121: kali9/iStockphoto/Getty Images, Free art director/iStockphoto/Getty Images; p. 122: HoaiPT/iStockphoto/Getty Images, Hajakely/iStockphoto/Getty Images, JianGang Wang/iStockphoto/Getty Images; p. 123: Brostock/iStockphoto/Getty Images, syolacan/iStockphoto/Getty Images; p. 126: flowgraph/iStockphoto/Getty Images, Silvrshootr/iStockphoto/Getty Images, Dreamstime/Glow Images, ugurhan/iStockphoto/Getty Images, sharrocks/iStockphoto/Getty Images, vinhdav/iStockphoto/Getty Images, IvancoVlad/iStockphoto/Getty Images, Coprid/iStockphoto/Getty Images, Tolga TEZCAN/iStockphoto/Getty Images, Udomsook/iStockphoto/Getty Images, Roman_Gorielov/iStockphoto/Getty Images, sunstock/iStockphoto/Getty Images, EkaterinaZakharova/iStockphoto/Getty Images, StratosGiannikos/iStockphoto/Getty Images, design56/iStockphoto/Getty Images, BWFolsom/iStockphoto/Getty Images; p. 127: flowgraph/iStockphoto/Getty Images, Getty Images, vinhdav/iStockphoto/Getty Images, Album/Fotoarena

Dados Internacionais de Catalogação na Publicação (CIP)
Bibliotecária responsável: Aline Graziele Benitez CRB-1/3129

C23n	Cant, Amanda
1.ed.	Next Station 3: Student's Book / Amanda Cant, Mary Charrington, Sarah Elizabeth Sprague; [Adapt.] Sue Clarke. – 1.ed. – São Paulo: Macmillan Education do Brasil, 2020.
	136 p.; il.; 21 x 27 cm. – (Coleção Next Station)
	ISBN: 978-85-511-0129-2
	1. Língua inglesa. I. Charrington, Mary. II. Sprague, Sarah Elizabeth. III. Clarke, Sue. IV. Título. V. Série.
	CDD 420

Índice para catálogo sistemático:
1. Língua inglesa

All rights reserved.

MACMILLAN EDUCATION DO BRASIL
Av. Brigadeiro Faria Lima, 1.309, 3º Andar –
Jd. Paulistano – São Paulo – SP – 01452-002
www.macmillan.com.br
Customer Service: [55] (11) 4613-2278
0800 16 88 77
Fax: [55] (11) 4612-6098

Printed in Brazil. Pancrom 10/2023

·MAP STICKERS·

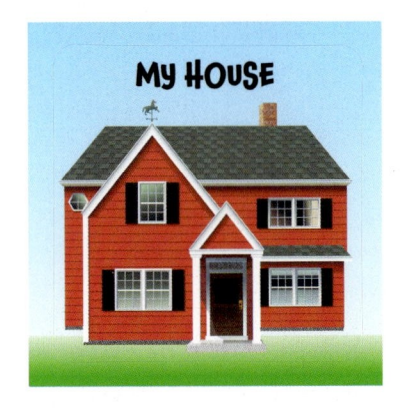

My House

INTERNATIONAL PASSPORT

Surname

Given Names

Passport No.
AA012345

Personal No.
0123456789

Date of birth

Sex

Date of issue

Holder's signature

Date of expiration

P<<<<<<<<<<<<<<<<<<<<<<<<<<<<<<<<<<<<<<<
AA012345<<<DDMMYY<<<AA012345<<<DDMMYY<<<<

ARRIVAL DATE:

___ /___ /_____

DEPARTURE DATE:

___ /___ /_____

MY LEARNING

	✓	?	✗
I can talk about what I like doing.			
I can talk about transportation.			
I can read and say words with *ar*, *all*, and *or*.			
I can describe myself and other people.			
I can describe where things or people are.			
I learned about iguanas in Mexico.			
I can talk about an animal from my country.			

ARRIVAL DATE:

___ /___ /_____

DEPARTURE DATE:

___ /___ /_____

MY LEARNING

I can express food likes and dislikes.	✓ ? ✗
I can say sentences with *There are some* and *There aren't any*.	✓ ? ✗
I can read and say words with *br*, *sn*, and *cl*.	✓ ? ✗
I can name foods.	✓ ? ✗
I can talk about food using *some* and *any*.	✓ ? ✗
I learned about food in South Africa.	✓ ? ✗
I can talk about a meal from my country.	✓ ? ✗

UNIT 3

ARRIVAL MALAYSIA 06 OCT

ARRIVAL DATE:

___ / ___ / _____

DEPARTURE DATE:

___ / ___ / _____

· MY LEARNING ·

I can talk about countries and nationalities.	✓ ? ✗
I can ask and answer where people are from.	✓ ? ✗
I can read and say words with *fr*, *bl*, and *lk*.	✓ ? ✗
I learned some action verbs.	✓ ? ✗
I can use *me*, *you*, *him*, *her*, *it*, *us*, *you* and *them*.	✓ ? ✗
I learned about the kite festival in Malaysia.	✓ ? ✗
I can talk about a festival from my country.	✓ ? ✗

ARRIVAL DATE:

___ /___ /_____

DEPARTURE DATE:

___ /___ /_____

· MY LEARNING ·

I can use sport verbs and talk about where to practice these sports.	✓ ? ✗
I can describe what people are doing.	✓ ? ✗
I can read and say words with *sk*, *sw*, and *str*.	✓ ? ✗
I can name some sports.	✓ ? ✗
I can ask and answer about what people are doing.	✓ ? ✗
I learned about soccer camps in Italy.	✓ ? ✗
I can talk about a popular sport in my country.	✓ ? ✗

ARRIVAL DATE:

___ /___ /_____

DEPARTURE DATE:

___ /___ /_____

MY LEARNING

I can talk about the weather.	✓ ? ✗
I can ask and answer about what *he*, *she*, *it* is doing.	✓ ? ✗
I can read and say words with *oo*, *ir*, and *ow*.	✓ ? ✗
I can say clothes words.	✓ ? ✗
I can ask and answer about what people are wearing or doing.	✓ ? ✗
I learned about the weather in Jamaica.	✓ ? ✗
I can talk about the weather in my country.	✓ ? ✗

ARRIVAL DATE:

___ /___ /_____

DEPARTURE DATE:

___ /___ /_____

MY LEARNING

I can name places in town.	✓	?	✗
I can ask and answer where *I*, *you*, *we*, *you*, *they* are going.	✓	?	✗
I can read and say words with *er*, *ear*, and *ore*.	✓	?	✗
I can name family members.	✓	?	✗
I can ask and answer where *he*, *she*, *it* is going.	✓	?	✗
I learned about a famous glacier in Chile.	✓	?	✗
I can talk about a special place in my country.	✓	?	✗

ARRIVAL DATE:

___ /___ /_____

DEPARTURE DATE:

___ /___ /_____

MY LEARNING

I can name jobs.	✓	?	✗
I can ask and answer about what people are going to be.	✓	?	✗
I can read and say words with *ur*, *or*, and *a*.	✓	?	✗
I can use verbs for daily routine activities.	✓	?	✗
I can talk about activities people are going to do.	✓	?	✗
I learned about ski schools in France.	✓	?	✗
I can talk about a teacher or instructor I admire.	✓	?	✗

UNIT 8

ARRIVAL DATE:

___ / ___ / _____

DEPARTURE DATE:

___ / ___ / _____

MY LEARNING

I can say the months and talk about birthdays.	✓ ? ✗
I can ask and answer about when and where people were born.	✓ ? ✗
I can read and say words with *dr*, *ld*, and *gr*.	✓ ? ✗
I can say how I was feeling.	✓ ? ✗
I can talk about the past.	✓ ? ✗
I learned about movie stars in the USA.	✓ ? ✗
I can talk about a famous actor.	✓ ? ✗

1974

2010

WELCOME TO MOROCCO INTERNATIONAL AIRPORT TOURISM 22 MAR

ARRIVAL DATE:

___ /___ /_____

DEPARTURE DATE:

___ /___ /_____

MY LEARNING

I can say the time.	✓ ? ✗
I can talk about where people were or weren't at different times.	✓ ? ✗
I can read and say words with *air*, *ou*, and *oy*.	✓ ? ✗
I can name special events.	✓ ? ✗
I can ask and answer about where people were.	✓ ? ✗
I learned about weddings in Morocco.	✓ ? ✗
I can talk about a special ceremony in my country.	✓ ? ✗

UNIT 10

WELCOME TO VIETNAM

ARRIVAL DATE:

___ /___ /_____

DEPARTURE DATE:

___ /___ /_____

MY LEARNING

I can name things in the house.	✓ ? ✗
I can talk about things I can or can't count in the past.	✓ ? ✗
I can read and say words with *sm*, *sc*, and *tr*.	✓ ? ✗
I can talk about seasons and the weather.	✓ ? ✗
I can ask question with *how much* and *how many* in the past.	✓ ? ✗
I learned about water puppets in Vietnam.	✓ ? ✗
I can talk about a traditional show from my country.	✓ ? ✗

21

spezi 044